Student Workbook

Environmental Science

Shoreview, Minnesota

ISBN 0-7854-3946-3

A 0 9 8 7 6 5 4 3 2 1

1-800-328-2560
www.agsglobe.com

Table of Contents

Table of Contents, continued

Table of Contents, continued

Introducing Environmental Science

Directions Choose the term from the Word Bank that completes each sentence correctly. Write the answer on the line.

Word Bank	
applied sciences	natural resources
environment	organisms
environmental science	

1. The _____ is an organism's natural and human-made surroundings.

2. Living things are known as _____.

3. Materials found in nature that are useful to humans are called _____.

4. The study of living things and how they interact with their environment is _____.

5. Fields of study that use scientific knowledge to solve practical problems are _____.

Directions Match the items in Column A with those in Column B. Write the letter of each correct answer on the line.

Column A

_____ 6. the study of how living things interact with the environment

_____ 7. the study of human societies

_____ 8. what humans have made, such as roads and buildings

_____ 9. the languages, religions, customs, and arts of a people

_____ 10. all the living and nonliving things found in nature

Column B

A anthropology

B built environment

C culture

D environmental science

E natural environment

A Living Planet

Directions Answer each question on the lines. Use complete sentences.

1. What are three things that people need to survive? _____

_____

2. Why do living things need energy? _____

_____

3. Where does most of Earth's energy come from? _____

_____

Directions Read each statement. Circle the answer that correctly completes each sentence.

4. A (pesticide, nutrient, pollutant) is a chemical used to control pests.

5. Oxygen will break apart, or (reproduce, dissolve, energize), in water.

6. Living things can (transpire, dissolve, reproduce), or breed and produce offspring.

7. (Wood, Metal, Oxygen) is an element all living things need to survive.

8. Each person needs about (1.9 liters, 1.9 gallons, 1.9 meters) of water a day to stay healthy.

9. The basic unit of life is a (molecule, cell, water), which makes up all living things.

10. Fish use organs called (lungs, cells, gills) to breathe underwater.

11. The ability to do work is (eating, energy, radiation).

12. Chemicals that organisms need to grow are called (nutrients, cells, waves).

13. Heat waves, light waves, and microwaves are all types of (nutrients, pesticides, electromagnetic radiation).

14. A (culture, nutrient, species) is a group of organisms that can breed together.

15. The gas that humans breathe out as waste is (oxygen, carbon dioxide, carbon monoxide).

A Short History of Life on Earth

Directions Choose the term from the Word Bank that completes each statement correctly. Write the answer on the line.

Word Bank		
agriculture	habitat	Industrial Revolution
Agricultural Revolution	*Homo sapiens*	landscape
cycle	hunter-gatherers	pollution

1. The environment where an animal lives is its _____.

2. People who survive by hunting animals and collecting food are _____.

3. Anything added to the environment that can harm living things is _____.

4. The scientific name for humans is _____.

5. Farming, or producing food crops, is also called _____.

6. The characteristics of the land are known as the _____.

7. The time in history when people began to farm and raise animals was the _____.

8. The time in history when people started using machines to produce products is the _____.

9. A(n) _____ is a repeating pattern.

Directions Answer each question on the lines. Use complete sentences.

10. When did the earliest life forms appear on Earth? _____

11. How long have humans been on Earth? _____

12. How did hunter-gatherers affect the environment? _____

13. How did the Agricultural Revolution change people's diets? _____

_____

14. What are some positive results of the Industrial Revolution? _____

_____

15. What is a harmful side effect of the Industrial Revolution? _____

_____

Introducing Environmental Challenges

Directions Unscramble the word or words in parentheses to complete each sentence. Write the answer on the line.

1. Pollution is one type, or _____, of environmental problem. (gayercot)

2. An example of a(n) _____ environmental problem is trash in a nearby park. (ollca)

3. Problems are described as _____ if they affect the whole world. (blaglo)

4. The earth has a lot of variety, or _____, but this is slowly being lost. (svtiiryde)

5. An oil spill off the eastern U.S. coast is an example of a(n) _____ pollution problem. (noeairlg)

Directions Write the letter of the answer that best completes each sentence.

6. Experts predict that by 2050, the Earth's population may grow to 9 _____ people.

   A thousand   **B** million   **C** billion   **D** trillion

7. The rise in global temperature is due in part to increased amounts of _____ gas in the air.

   A carbon dioxide   **B** oxygen   **C** hydrogen   **D** methane

8. One person in _____ uses more resources than one person in any other country.

   A China   **B** the United States   **C** India   **D** Spain

9. For most of human history, people have believed the earth had _____ resources.

   A limited   **B** unlimited   **C** not enough   **D** sparse

10. In a(n) _____ society, natural resources are preserved for future generations.

    A industrial   **B** hunter-gatherer   **C** sustainable   **D** global

How Science Works

Directions Match the items in Column A with those in Column B. Write the letter of each correct answer on the line.

Column A

_____ **1.** a personal belief that can affect an experiment's results

_____ **2.** a magazine in which scientists can share their data

_____ **3.** tiny organisms that make their own food

_____ **4.** what is tested in an experiment

_____ **5.** a study done in a natural environment

_____ **6.** information collected and organized during an experiment

_____ **7.** the process of making sense of an experiment's results

_____ **8.** a group in an experiment that has no variable changed

_____ **9.** a group in an experiment with one variable changed that is being tested

_____ **10.** an educated guess

_____ **11.** worldwide network of computers where scientific information can be shared

Column B

A algae

B analysis

C bias

D control group

E data

F experimental group

G field study

H hypothesis

I Internet

J scientific journal

K variable

Directions Answer each question on the lines. Use complete sentences.

12. What is meant by coral bleaching? _____

_____

13. What are the steps of the scientific method? _____

_____

14. Why do scientists perform their experiments many times? _____

_____

15. Why is it vital that scientists publish and share their data? _____

_____

_____

Science and Society

Directions Answer each question on the lines. Use complete sentences.

1. Why is science important to human society? _____

_____

2. List some characteristics of a good scientist. _____

_____

3. What does being skeptical mean? _____

_____

4. Why are ethics an important part of science? _____

_____

5. What kinds of issues can environmental justice help to solve? _____

_____

Directions Write the word or words that complete each sentence correctly.

6. A(n) _____ is a well-tested hypothesis that explains many scientific observations.

7. A(n) _____ is a statement of a basic law or truth.

8. _____ help a person decide between right and wrong.

9. The effects of different actions are called _____.

10. Dealing with environmental problems in a way that treats everyone equally is known as _____.

Directions Classify each concept as objective or subjective. Write *O* for objective and *S* for subjective.

11.	Facts and scientific measurements	
12.	Love of art, music, and literature	
13.	Personal feelings	
14.	Data collected from experiments	
15.	Opinions	

Chapter 1 Vocabulary Review

Directions Match the items in Column A with those in Column B. Write the letter of each correct answer on the line.

Column A

_____ **1.** materials found in nature that are useful to people

_____ **2.** affecting part of the world

_____ **3.** dealing with environmental problems in a way that treats everyone equally

_____ **4.** the group in an experiment where nothing is changed

_____ **5.** the things that humans have made

_____ **6.** a group

_____ **7.** all of the living and nonliving things in an area

_____ **8.** a science magazine

_____ **9.** the variety of life on Earth

_____ **10.** provides practical solutions to problems using scientific knowledge

_____ **11.** a repeating pattern

_____ **12.** not influenced by personal feelings or opinions

_____ **13.** variety

_____ **14.** set of principles that help determine right from wrong

_____ **15.** the ability to do work

Column B

A built environment

B control group

C environmental justice

D natural resources

E regional

F applied science

G biodiversity

H category

I ecosystem

J scientific journal

K cycle

L diversity

M energy

N morals

O objective

Chapter 1 Vocabulary Review, continued

Column A

Column B

_____ **16.** a time when people started using machines to produce products

_____ **17.** electric and magnetic waves

_____ **18.** farming

_____ **19.** a person who survives by moving from place to place, hunting and gathering food

_____ **20.** the environment where an organism lives

P agriculture

Q electromagnetic radiation

R habitat

S hunter-gatherer

T Industrial Revolution

_____ **21.** help a person to decide between right and wrong

_____ **22.** only affecting a certain place

_____ **23.** the languages, religions, customs, arts, and dress of a group of people

_____ **24.** the scientific name for modern humans

_____ **25.** a basic law or truth

_____ **26.** a time when hunter-gatherers began farming and raising animals for food

U Agricultural Revolution

V culture

W ethics

X _Homo sapiens_

Y local

Z principle

Directions Unscramble the word or words in parentheses to complete each sentence. Write the answer on the line.

27. The _____ includes all things that are found in nature. (ltanrua noevetrinmn)

28. A problem that is _____ affects the whole world. (lbogla)

29. When a person is _____, they question what they read or hear. (pikalcest)

30. Living things are harmed when _____ is added to the environment. (lunopolit)

31. A(n) _____ is the basic unit of life. (lcle)

32. A scientist conducts a(n) _____ outdoors. (lifed yudts)

Chapter 1 Vocabulary Review, continued

33. A well-tested hypothesis that explains many scientific observations is called a(n) _____. (rehoyt)

34. The chemicals organisms need to grow are called _____. (rittnenus)

35. When an organism becomes _____, it no longer exists. (nixctet)

36. An organism's _____ includes the natural and human-made things that surround it. (vemnrntieno)

37. During _____, a coral will turn white and die. (olrac higlebanc)

38. A(n) _____ is the part that is changed in an experiment. (bavleria)

39. When an organism _____, it breeds and produces offspring. (porudecrse)

40. Personal feelings and opinions are _____. (tijbuescev)

41. In a(n) _____, natural resources are preserved for future generations. (tbsinaeslua iosctye)

42. The rise in world temperatures is also known as _____. (llogba granwmi)

Directions Write the letter of the answer that best completes each sentence.

43. When something _____, it breaks apart.

A dissolves **B** absorbs **C** combines **D** heats

44. A(n) _____ is a chemical used to kill or control pests.

A fertilizer **B** disinfectant **C** pesticide **D** herbicide

45. All living things are called _____.

A life forms **B** organisms **C** animals **D** species

46. If a person is _____, their beliefs may affect the results of an experiment.

A careless **B** opinionated **C** judgmental **D** biased

47. A _____ is a group of organisms that can breed with each other.

A species **B** family **C** group **D** kingdom

Chapter 1 Vocabulary Review, continued

48. The _____ is the group in an experiment where one part is changed.

    A control group   **B** hypothesis   **C** variable   **D** experimental group

49. The process of making sense of an experiment's results is called _____.

    A hypothesis   **B** analysis   **C** experimentation   **D** data collection

50. A _____ is an educated guess.

    A theory   **B** principle   **C** hypothesis   **D** trial

51. The study of how living things affect their environment is called _____.

    A natural science   **B** eco-science   **C** life science   **D** environmental science

52. A _____ is the effect of an action.

    A cause   **B** value   **C** bias   **D** consequence

53. The _____ is used to test possible answers to scientific questions.

    A experimental data   **B** scientific method   **C** variable method   **D** experimental group

54. The characteristics of the land in an area are part of the _____.

    A landscape   **B** ecosystem   **C** environment   **D** community

55. During a scientific experiment, _____ is collected and recorded.

    A energy   **B** data   **C** analysis   **D** a hypothesis

56. The _____ is a worldwide network of computers.

    A computer web   **B** data system   **C** world net   **D** Internet

57. Tiny organisms that make their own food are called _____.

    A bacteria   **B** coral   **C** algae   **D** insects

58. _____ are what are important to a person.

    A Theories   **B** Values   **C** Religions   **D** Cultures

59. _____ takes place when resources are used faster than they can be replaced.

    A Environmental justice   **C** Overconsumption
    B Coral bleaching   **D** Environmental science

60. Something that is _____ is made in large quantities.

    A skeptical   **B** massive   **C** global   **D** mass-produced

The Earth Forms

Directions Read the sentences. Put the steps of how the earth formed in order.
Write 1, 2, 3, or 4 on the line in front of each sentence.

_____ **1.** Energy heated the new planet to high temperatures.

_____ **2.** Earth's molten surface hardened into rock.

_____ **3.** The earth began to cool.

_____ **4.** Gas and rocky debris circling the sun crashed together.

Directions Complete the science terms by writing missing letters.
Use the clues to help you.

5. lighter crust

c		n	t		n		n	t		l

6. heavier crust

		c			n		c

Directions Choose the term from the Word Bank that completes each sentence
correctly. Write your answer on the line.

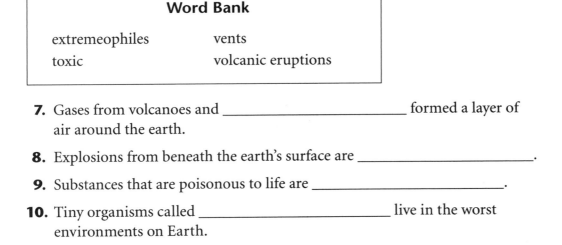

Word Bank	
extremeophiles	vents
toxic	volcanic eruptions

7. Gases from volcanoes and _____ formed a layer of
air around the earth.

8. Explosions from beneath the earth's surface are _____.

9. Substances that are poisonous to life are _____.

10. Tiny organisms called _____ live in the worst
environments on Earth.

Land, Water, and Air

Directions Use the terms in the Word Bank to complete the paragraph. Write the terms on the lines.

Word Bank			
atmosphere	biosphere	hydrosphere	lithosphere

The **1.** _____ is Earth's solid surface and interior.

The liquid layer where the earth's water is found is the **2.** _____ .

The **3.** _____ is the layer of air that surrounds the

earth. Life can be found in parts of all three layers. Together, these parts

are known as Earth's **4.** _____ .

Directions When you compare and contrast, you tell how things are alike and how they are different. Compare and contrast the pairs of words below.

  5. plate tectonics and continental drift

   A How they are alike: _____

   B How they are different: _____

  6. atmosphere and hydrosphere

   A How they are alike: _____

   B How they are different: _____

Directions Unscramble the word or words in parentheses to complete each sentence. Write the answer on the line.

  7. The hydrosphere includes _____, which is water found underground. (wgdnruotrea)

  8. Water helps _____, or chemical changes, take place. (lhmeccai stnoircea)

  9. Water in the form of a gas is also called water _____. (proav)

  10. The _____ protects Earth from harmful ultraviolet radiation. (nzoeo ralye)

Cycles of Life

Directions Read each statement. Circle the answer that correctly completes each sentence.

1. Bacteria change nitrogen in the air into (elements, calcium, nitrates).

2. In the (carbon cycle, oxygen cycle, water cycle), water moves from the air to the earth and back to the air.

3. (Evaporation, Condensation, Precipitation) is the process of water changing from a liquid to a gas.

4. (Evaporation, Precipitation, Condensation) occurs when water changes from vapor to a liquid.

5. (Condensation, Precipitation, Transpiration) is water falling to Earth from the atmosphere as rain, hail, sleet, or snow.

Directions Choose the term from the Word Bank that completes each sentence correctly. Write the answer on the line.

Word Bank				
ammonium	carbon dioxide	oxygen	particle	polar ice caps

6. When you breathe, you take in _____ and give off carbon dioxide.

7. The enormous masses of ice at the North and South Poles are _____.

8. A tiny piece of matter, like an atom, is a(n) _____.

9. Many plants can use nitrogen in the form of _____.

10. Plants take in the gas _____ and use it to make sugar.

Climate and Weather

Directions Match the items in Column A with those in Column B.
Write the letter of the correct answer on the line.

Column A

_____ **1.** to turn in a circle

_____ **2.** moment-by-moment conditions in the atmosphere

_____ **3.** move in a circle around a point

_____ **4.** a straight line that an object seems to rotate around

_____ **5.** the average weather in a particular area

_____ **6.** areas of land lying near the equator

_____ **7.** parts of the world north of the equator

_____ **8.** an imaginary line halfway between the North
and South Poles

_____ **9.** parts of the world south of the equator

_____ **10.** the amount of water vapor in the air

Column B

A axis

B climate

C equator

D humidity

E Northern Hemisphere

F revolve

G rotate

H Southern Hemisphere

I tropics

J weather

Directions Answer each question on the lines. Use complete sentences.

11. What are prevailing winds? Give three examples. _____

_____

12. What are jet streams? _____

_____

13. Define air pressure. _____

_____

14. Explain the Coriolis effect. _____

_____

15. How does climate affect where organisms live? _____

_____

_____

Our Changing World

Directions Write the letter of the answer that best completes each sentence.

1. _____ are long, cold periods in Earth's history.

   A Glaciers   **B** Pangaea   **C** Ice ages   **D** Rotations

2. Scientists use radioactive elements called _____ to determine the age of rocks.

   A radioisotopes   **B** atoms   **C** radio waves   **D** fossils

3. Preserved traces or remains of plants and animals are called _____.

   A radioisotopes   **B** fossils   **C** glaciers   **D** rocks

4. _____ rocks are made up of layers of sand, gravel, and mud.

   A Fossilized   **B** Radioactive   **C** Sedimentary   **D** Proxy

5. Masses of ice that move over land are called _____.

   A glaciers   **B** fossils   **C** sediments   **D** hail

6. The sources, or _____, of rocks give clues to the earth's past.

   A fossils   **B** radioisotopes   **C** origins   **D** sediments

7. Earth's _____ causes day and night.

   A radiation   **B** rotation   **C** precipitation   **D** revolution

8. Information that is not as precise as instrument readings is called _____ data.

   A proxy   **B** constructed   **C** radiometric   **D** global

9. At one time, Earth had a single landmass called _____.

   A Pangaea   **C** the North Pole
   B the polar ice cap   **D** plate tectonics

Directions Some changes happen quickly and are easy to notice. Other changes occur slowly and are hard to notice. Write *F* on the line if the environmental change happens fast. Write *S* on the line if the change is slow.

_____ **10.** Earth's rotation on its axis   _____ **13.** weather changes

_____ **11.** movement of Earth's plates   _____ **14.** global climate changes

_____ **12.** the water cycle   _____ **15.** mountain formation

Chapter 2 Vocabulary Review

Directions Write the letter of the answer that best completes each sentence.

1. When something is _____, it has melted into a liquid.

  A flowing   **B** molten   **C** condensed   **D** vaporized

2. The moment-by-moment conditions in an area are called the _____.

  A climate   **B** temperature   **C** atmosphere   **D** weather

3. The _____ is the layer of air surrounding the earth.

  A atmosphere   **B** hydrosphere   **C** lithosphere   **D** hemisphere

4. Water or other materials in gas form are called _____.

  A liquids   **B** vapors   **C** solids   **D** particles

5. The _____ is where life can be found on Earth.

  A biosphere   **B** thermosphere   **C** land   **D** core

6. A _____ is a frozen mass that orbits the sun.

  A meteor   **B** moon   **C** star   **D** comet

7. The _____ are near the equator.

  A ice caps   **B** temperate regions   **C** tropics   **D** North and South Poles

8. The hot center of the earth is called the _____.

  A axis   **B** core   **C** mantle   **D** crust

9. When something _____, it moves in a circle around a point.

  A rotates   **B** turns   **C** revolves   **D** cycles

10. The _____ theory describes how continents move over time.

  A Pangaea   **B** shifting land   **C** floating continent   **D** continental drift

11. Basic building blocks of matter are called _____.

  A elements   **B** atoms   **C** minerals   **D** nutrients

12. The _____ is the layer of air people live and breathe in.

  A troposhere   **B** mesosphere   **C** thermosphere   **D** stratosphere

Chapter 2 Vocabulary Review, continued

13. The _____ is the source or beginning of something.

A climax   **B** finale   **C** origin   **D** conclusion

14. The process of changing from liquid to vapor is called _____.

A transpiration   **B** respiation   **C** melting   **D** evaporation

15. A tiny piece of something is a(n) _____.

A element   **B** particle   **C** compound   **D** pinnacle

16. The earth's surface layer of rock and soil is called the _____.

A crust   **B** core   **C** vent   **D** mantle

17. _____ was the single landmass on Earth 200 million years ago.

A Eurasia   **B** Pandemic   **C** Americana   **D** Pangaea

18. The _____ protects Earth from harmful solar rays.

A stratosphere   **B** jet stream   **C** ozone layer   **D** thermosphere

19. A(n) _____ is a trace of a plant or animal preserved in rock.

A artifact   **B** fossil   **C** skeleton   **D** preserves

20. To _____ is to turn in a circle.

A revolve   **B** swirl   **C** rotate   **D** flip

Directions Match the items in Column A with those in Column B.
Write the letter of each correct answer on the line.

Column A	Column B
_____ **21.** the process of water moving from the air to Earth and back to the air	**A** life-support system
_____ **22.** a system that provides everything needed to stay alive	**B** mesosphere
_____ **23.** layer of the earth's atmosphere between the stratosphere and the thermosphere	**C** Northern Hemisphere
_____ **24.** study of how the earth's plates move	**D** plate tectonics
_____ **25.** parts of the world north of the equator	**E** water cycle

Chapter 2 Vocabulary Review, continued

Column A		Column B

Column A

_____ **26.** lighter part of the earth's crust; makes up continents

_____ **27.** water changing from vapor to liquid

_____ **28.** a chemical change

_____ **29.** imaginary line halfway between the North and South Poles

_____ **30.** straight line that an object rotates around

_____ **31.** blue-green algae

_____ **32.** three major wind belts on Earth

_____ **33.** layered rocks formed by sand, gravel, and mud

_____ **34.** high-energy radiation from the sun

_____ **35.** elements that help determine the age of rocks

_____ **36.** wind patterns caused by the rotation of the earth

_____ **37.** a tiny organism that lives in harsh environments

_____ **38.** parts of the world south of the equator

_____ **39.** water moving from the inside of a plant into the atmosphere

_____ **40.** a period of global cooling

_____ **41.** the solid surface and interior of the earth

_____ **42.** a form of nitrogen that most plants can absorb

_____ **43.** pressure caused by the weight of the atmosphere

_____ **44.** the water layer of the earth

_____ **45.** masses of ice at the North and South Poles

_____ **46.** water found underground

Column B

F axis

G chemical reaction

H condensation

I continental crust

J equator

K cyanobacteria

L prevailing winds

M radioisotopes

N sedimentary rocks

O ultraviolet radiation

P Coriolis effect

Q extremeophile

R ice age

S Southern Hemisphere

T transpiration

U air pressure

V groundwater

W hydrosphere

X lithosphere

Y nitrate

Z polar ice caps

Chapter 2 Vocabulary Review, continued

Directions Unscramble the word or words in parentheses to complete each sentence. Write the answer on the line.

47. The remains of something that was destroyed is called _____. (sbedir)

48. A(n) _____ is a piece of rock that hits a planet. (eeeorimtt)

49. The _____ is the layer of the earth surrounding the core. (lemnta)

50. The average weather of an area is the _____. (teimacl)

51. Rain, hail, sleet, and snow are types of _____. (itpicnoreptia)

52. The _____ is above the troposphere. (tossaheprret)

53. Large masses of ice called _____ move over land. (caglesri)

54. When something is _____, it is poisonous. (xcoti)

55. The _____ is a strong air current high in the atmosphere. (tje rmeast)

56. A(n) _____ is an opening in the earth. (netv)

57. The smallest organisms on Earth are _____. (ceabarit)

58. Earth's past climate can be studied using fossilized evidence called _____. (xorpy taad)

59. The _____ makes up the ocean floor. (naccoei urtcs)

60. A(n) _____ has only one kind of atom. (letemne)

61. Some plants can absorb nitrogen in the form of _____. (miummano)

62. A(n) _____ is an explosion from beneath the earth's surface. (prutoeni)

63. The amount of moisture in the air is known as _____. (dmiityuh)

64. The layer of atmosphere above the mesosphere is the _____. (hoetepserhmr)

Everything Is Connected

Directions When you compare and contrast, you tell how things are
alike and how they are different. Compare and contrast each pair below.

1. ecology and ecologist

    A How they are alike: _____

    B How they are different: _____

2. biotic factors and abiotic factors

    A How they are alike: _____

    B How they are different: _____

3. domains and kingdoms

    A How they are alike: _____

    B How they are different: _____

Directions Use the terms in the Word Bank to complete the paragraph.
Write the terms on the lines.

Word Bank			
banned	DDT	pesticides	strong
crushed	disappearing	poisoned	

In the 1960s, scientists noticed that peregrine falcons were **4.** _____.

After studying the problem, they discovered that a chemical pesticide called

5. _____ was responsible. Farmers use **6.** _____

to kill the insects that feed on their crops. When birds ate insects containing

DDT, the chemical **7.** _____ them. When peregrine

falcons ate the poisoned birds, DDT built up in their bodies. DDT prevented

females from laying eggs with **8.** _____ shells. The weight

of the parents **9.** _____ the eggs, and the chicks died.

Eventually, DDT was **10.** _____, and bird populations

started to recover.

Components of an Ecosystem

Directions Use the clues to complete the word or words below it.

1. group of different species that live and interact in the same area

c		m	m		n		t	y

2. all of the earth's ecosystems

b			s	p	h		r	

3. the creation of new life

r		p	r		d		c	t			n

4. made up of living and nonliving factors that interact

	c		s	y	s	t		m

5. members of the same species living in one area

p		p		l		t			n

6. to use the same matter many times and in many different forms

r		c	y	c	l	

7. a combination of several atoms

m		l		c		l	

Directions Answer each question on the line. Use complete sentences.

8. What two jobs do all ecosystems share? _____

_____

9. Ecosystems get almost all of their energy from what source? _____

_____

10. What is cellular respiration? _____

_____

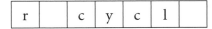

Producers, Consumers, and Decomposers

Directions Complete the table. Write the letter of the correct word on the line.

A consumer   **D** lion
B decomposer   **E** producer
C grass

Types of Organism	Process of Getting Food	Examples of Organism
1. _____	Capture the sun's energy	**2.** _____
3. _____	Eats producers and other consumers	**4.** _____
5. _____	Breaks down dead organisms and other organic wastes	Fungi

Directions Unscramble the word in parentheses to complete each sentence. Write the answer on the line.

6. In the process of _____, some organisms use chemicals to create nutrients. (nsyssethoheimc)

7. Molecules that do not contain carbon atoms are described as _____. (gironinca)

8. Carbon-containing matter that is alive or was once alive is called _____ matter. (gcinoar)

9. A(n) _____ is an animal that feeds on dead animals or plants. (vnerasgce)

10. In plants, the green pigment _____ absorbs sunlight. (lolyrclohph)

Energy Flow in Ecosystems

Directions Choose the term from the Word Bank that completes each sentence correctly. Write the answer on the line.

Word Bank	
energy pyramid	tertiary consumer(s)
primary consumer(s)	trophic level
secondary consumer(s)	

1. A(n) _____ shows how energy is transferred from one trophic level to the next.

2. A(n) _____ is a feeding level in a food chain or food web.

3. Carnivores that feed on other carnivores are called _____.

4. Carnivores that feed on herbivores are called _____.

5. Herbivores that feed on plants are _____.

Directions Answer each question on the lines. Use complete sentences.

6. What are three examples of secondary consumers? _____

_____

7. Why are there more producers than consumers in an ecosystem?

_____

_____

8. How does a food web differ from a food chain? _____

_____

9. Describe the path of energy through a food chain. _____

_____

10. On what resource do all organisms in an ecosystem depend on for energy?

_____

_____

Relationships Within Ecosystems

Directions Choose the term from the Word Bank that completes each sentence correctly. Write the answer on the line.

Word Bank		
camouflage	mimicry	predation
competition	niche	prey

1. In _____, one organism hunts and feeds on another organism.

2. Some species use _____—colors, patterns, or behaviors—to prevent being eaten.

3. The animal that a predator feeds on is called its _____.

4. A _____ is the role an organism plays in its ecosystem.

5. When two species try to use the same resource, _____ occurs.

6. Some species use _____ to look like or act like a more dangerous species.

Directions Answer each question on the lines. Use complete sentences.

7. How does competition affect a community? _____

_____

8. How are an organism's habitat and niche related? _____

_____

9. Name two ways prey protect themselves from predators. _____

_____

10. Bats and dragonflies both eat mosquitoes but are not in competition. Explain why.

_____

_____

Ecosystems and Change

Directions Read each statement. Circle the answer that correctly completes each sentence.

1. The process of change in an ecosystem over time is called (distribution, climax community, succession).

2. In (secondary succession, primary succession, distribution), a lifeless environment develops into a community.

3. Changes in communities that have been disturbed by humans or natural disasters are (secondary succession, primary succession, distribution).

4. The last step in the succession of an ecosystem is called a(n) (old-growth forest, distribution, climax community).

5. A(n) (climax community, old-growth forest, pioneer species) contains trees that may be hundreds of years old.

Directions Match the items in Column A with those in Column B. Write the letter of the correct answer on the line.

Column A	Column B
_____ **6.** to break apart or wear away	**A** distribution
_____ **7.** the first species to arrive in an area	**B** diverse
_____ **8.** varied or containing many different organisms	**C** erode
_____ **9.** the arrangement of species in a community	**D** lichen
_____ **10.** an organism made of a fungus, a green alga, and a cyanobacterium	**E** pioneer species

Directions Complete the chart. Write *P* in the last column to indicate primary succession. Write *S* to indicate secondary succession.

Statement	Type of Succession
11. New volcanic island	
12. Pioneer species	
13. After a flood or a fire	
14. Succession in a lifeless environment	
15. When farmland is abandoned	

Chapter 3 Vocabulary Review

Directions Match the items in Column A with those in Column B.
Write the letter of each correct answer on the line.

Column A

_____ **1.** carnivores that feed on herbivores

_____ **2.** nonliving substance important to human health

_____ **3.** bright colors or patterns to scare off predators

_____ **4.** an organism that makes its own food

_____ **5.** a dead animal or rotten meat

_____ **6.** cycle showing how predator and prey populations are linked

_____ **7.** to forbid by law

_____ **8.** feeding order of organisms in a community

_____ **9.** using the same matter many times in different forms

_____ **10.** a feeding level in a food chain

_____ **11.** living things that must be magnified to be seen

_____ **12.** process of natural change in an ecosystem over time

_____ **13.** organism that feeds on other organisms

_____ **14.** living or dead materials that contain carbon

_____ **15.** combination of several atoms

_____ **16.** three largest groups of similar organisms

_____ **17.** food

_____ **18.** chemical that absorbs certain kinds of light energy

_____ **19.** diagram that shows the amount of energy in different trophic levels

_____ **20.** the creation of new life

Column B

A carrion

B mineral

C producer

D secondary consumer

E warning coloration

F ban

G boom-bust cycle

H food chain

I recycle

J trophic level

K consumer

L microorganism

M molecule

N organic

O succession

P domain

Q energy pyramid

R nourishment

S pigment

T reproduction

Chapter 3 Vocabulary Review, continued

Column A

_____ **21.** members of one species living in the same area

_____ **22.** living part of the environment

_____ **23.** contains trees that can be hundreds of years old

_____ **24.** an organism's role in an ecosystem

_____ **25.** creating energy from chemicals

_____ **26.** animal that feeds on dead plants or animals

Column B

U biotic factor

V chemosynthesis

W niche

X old-growth forest

Y population

Z scavenger

Directions Read each statement. Circle the answer that correctly completes each sentence.

27. The arrangement of species in a community is known as (succession, distribution, diversity).

28. When organisms (adapt, camouflage, coexist), they exist at the same time in the same place.

29. A(n) (community, ecosystem, biosphere) is made up of different populations interacting in an area.

30. Herbivores that feed on plants are called (primary consumers, secondary consumers, tertiary consumers).

31. A(n) (organic, biotic, inorganic) substance does not contain carbon.

32. Succession that occurs in an uninhabited place is (distribution, primary succession, secondary succession).

33. When an organism has (camouflage, warning coloration, mimicry), it can blend in and hide from predators.

34. The last step in the succession of an ecosystem is a (pioneer species, trophic level, climax community).

35. When all the food chains in a community are linked together, it creates a(n) (energy pyramid, food web, trophic level).

36. The study of how living things interact with each other and the environment is (biology, botany, ecology).

37. A(n) (prey, herbivore, predator) hunts and feeds on other consumers.

38. An animal that eats both plants and animals is a(n) (herbivore, omnivore, carnivore).

Chapter 3 Vocabulary Review, continued

39. Cells use (photosynthesis, cellular respiration, chemosynthesis) to produce energy from carbohydrates.

40. (Lichens, Omnivores, Decomposers) are organisms made up of fungi, green algae, and cyanobacteria.

41. A consumer that is eaten by a predator is (competition, niche, prey).

42. To break apart or wear away is to (erode, erupt, deposit).

43. A(n) (microorganism, abiotic factor, biotic factor) is a nonliving part of the environment.

44. When individuals try to use the same limited resources, there is (predation, competition, succession).

45. Plants contain a green pigment called (chlorophyll, chloroplast, carbon dioxide), which absorbs sunlight.

46. A(n) (herbivore, omnivore, carnivore) only eats plants.

Directions Write the letter of the correct answer on the line.

47. Organisms that break down organic matter are _____.

   A decomposers   **B** producers   **C** consumers   **D** scavengers

48. A(n) _____ is a scientist who studies ecology.

   A zoologist   **B** biologist   **C** geneticist   **D** ecologist

49. A(n) _____ is a carnivore that feeds on other carnivores.

   A primary consumer   **C** tertiary consumer
   B secondary consumer   **D** producer

50. The first species to arrive in an area are called _____.

   A abiotic factors   **C** producers
   B pioneer species   **D** primary consumers

51. The process plants use to change the sun's energy into sugars is called _____.

   A chemosynthesis   **C** transformation
   B photosynthesis   **D** decomposition

52. A(n) _____ is an animal that eats other animals.

   A producer   **B** carnivore   **C** herbivore   **D** omnivore

Chapter 3 Vocabulary Review, continued

53. Changes that occur in ecosystems that have been disturbed are a result of _____.

    A primary succession   **C** decomposition

    B secondary succession   **D** erosion

54. A level of classification inside a domain is known as a(n) _____.

    A kingdom   **B** ecosystem   **C** dominion   **D** classification

55. When a predator hunts and eats its prey it is called _____.

    A succession   **B** predation   **C** selection   **D** mimicry

56. When a habitat is _____, it has many varied species.

    A disturbed   **B** organic   **C** diverse   **D** successional

57. In _____, one species looks, sounds, or acts like a more dangerous species.

    A camouflage   **C** warning coloration

    B mimicry   **D** predator

58. The structures in plant cells that contain chlorophyll are _____.

    A roots   **B** cells   **C** cultures   **D** chloroplasts

59. Chemistry is the study of _____ and its changes.

    A matter   **B** the environment   **C** animals   **D** plants

Introducing Biodiversity

Directions Complete the table. Write the letter of the correct description or example on the line.

    A Deserts, grasslands, and swamps   **D** Eastern bluebirds, African lions, and great white sharks
    B Ecosystem   **E** Variety of genes in living things
    C Species

Types of Biodiversity	Definition	Examples
1. _____	Variety of species on Earth	**2.** _____
Genetic	**3.** _____	Hair color and eye color
4. _____	Variety of ecosystems on Earth	**5.** _____

Directions Write the letter of the answer that best completes each sentence.

6. A _____ is passed from parent to offspring. It carries information about a trait.
    A species   **B** culture   **C** biotic factor   **D** gene

7. An inherited characteristic, like brown eyes, is a(n) _____.
    A trait   **B** ethic   **C** organism   **D** variable

8. The protection of natural resources is _____.
    A ecology   **B** conservation   **C** biology   **D** biodiversity

Directions When you compare and contrast, you tell how things are alike and how they are different. Compare and contrast each pair below.

9. biologist and conservationist

    A How they are alike: _____

    _____

    B How they are different: _____

    _____

10. species diversity and genetic diversity

    A How they are alike: _____

    _____

    B How they are different: _____

    _____

Measuring Diversity

Directions Choose the term from the Word Bank that completes each sentence correctly. Write the answer on the line.

Word Bank		
endangered	invertebrate	specimen
endemic	mass extinction	taxonomy
extinction		

1. The loss of all members of a species is _____.

2. An animal that does not have a backbone is a(n) _____.

3. During a(n) _____, a large number of species becomes extinct.

4. A(n) _____ species is found in one part of the world and nowhere else.

5. In the branch of science called _____, scientists classify species.

6. Species that are _____ are in danger of extinction.

Directions Answer each question on the line. Use complete sentences.

7. How many species of living things have been identified worldwide?

_____

8. Why do scientists not know the exact number of species on Earth?

_____

_____

9. Why might a scientist collect a specimen of a species?

_____

_____

10. How can samples help scientists estimate the total number of species on Earth?

_____

_____

Evolution and Adaptation

Directions Use the clue to complete the word below it.

1. The process of genetic change in a population over time is _____.

	v		l		t			n

2. Animals of the same species may be separated by a physical barrier. If this happens, the animals cannot _____, or breed together.

	n	t		r	b	r			d

3. A trait that helps an organism survive in its environment is a(n) _____.

	d		p	t		t	i		n

4. The evolution of a new species is _____.

	p		c			t		n

5. Species can _____, or develop genetically over time.

	v		l	v	

Directions Match the items in Column A with those in Column B. Write the letter of each correct answer on the line.

Column A

_____ **6.** organisms best suited to the environment pass these to their offspring

_____ **7.** location visited by Charles Darwin in 1835

_____ **8.** to breed together

_____ **9.** birds studied by Darwin on his travels

_____ **10.** a sudden change in an organism's genes

Column B

A finches

B Galápagos Islands

C genes

D interbreed

E mutation

A Web of Life

Directions Choose the term from the Word Bank that completes each sentence correctly. Write the answer on the line.

Word Bank			
host	mutualism	parasite	symbiosis
keystone	nectar	pollination	tentacle

1. An armlike body part used to capture food is a _____.

2. A relationship between two species where both benefit is _____.

3. A _____ absorbs food from a host and harms it.

4. During _____, pollen is transferred between plants.

5. A _____ species adds to the diversity of the ecosystem.

6. Many flowers produce _____, a sweet liquid.

7. A _____ provides food for a parasite.

8. A close relationship between two species is _____.

Directions Answer each question on the lines. Use complete sentences.

9. What is pollen? _____

10. How do animals help some plants disperse their seeds? _____

11. Name two types of symbiosis. _____

12. Define parasitism. _____

13. Why are beavers a keystone species? _____

14. Explain commensalism. _____

15. How can the loss of one species affect many other species? _____

_____

The Benefits of Biodiversity

Directions Use the terms in the Word Bank to complete the paragraph.
Write the terms on the lines.

Word Bank		
compounds	ecosystem service	genetic diversity
economy	eroding	staple crop

A(n) **1.**_____ is a benefit provided by Earth's ecosystems.

Plants and animals provide ecosystem services. Plants make oxygen and food.

The roots of plants hold soil and stop it from **2.** _____.

Animals support ecosystems in many ways. Insects and other animals

pollinate plants. Plants that provide a basic part of many people's diets are called

3. _____. Wild plants have more **4.** _____

than tame ones. They can be used to improve crops like tomatoes. People also

benefit from natural materials that are medicines. Some natural **5.**_____,

combinations of two or more elements, help save lives. Medicine is part of the

global **6.** _____, a system of production, distribution,

and consumption.

Directions Unscramble the word or words in parentheses to
complete each sentence. Write the answer on the line.

7. People in _____ areas live inside the city. (arnub)

8. The earth's many natural resources are due to its rich
_____. (sivtridyeibo)

9. Areas away from the city are described as _____.
(ulrra)

10. People depend on the _____ produced by plants to
breathe. (nexgoy)

Chapter 4 Vocabulary Review

Directions Write the letter of the answer that best completes each sentence.

1. Areas away from a city are called _____.
   A urban   **B** rural   **C** northern   **D** distant

2. _____ is a branch of science dealing with the classification of species.
   A Ecology   **B** Chemistry   **C** Biology   **D** Taxonomy

3. In _____, one species benefits and the other is not affected.
   A mutualism   **B** parasitism   **C** commensalism   **D** predation

4. The evolution of a new species is called _____.
   A mutualism   **B** speciation   **C** interbreeding   **D** distinction

5. A(n) _____ species is only found in one part of the planet.
   A endemic   **B** pandemic   **C** local   **D** extinct

6. Species without backbones are called _____.
   A vertebrates   **B** reptiles   **C** invertebrates   **D** mammals

7. A(n) _____ is a combination of two or more elements.
   A mineral   **B** atom   **C** cell   **D** compound

8. To _____ is to develop and change genetically.
   A distinct   **B** interbreed   **C** evolve   **D** migrate

9. The variety of genes found in living things is called _____.
   A species diversity   **B** genetic diversity   **C** trait variation   **D** gene pool

10. A _____ is an armlike body part used to capture food.
    A ganglia   **B** tentacle   **C** tail   **D** radula

11. In _____, one species benefits and the other is harmed.
    A mutualism   **B** commensalism   **C** parasitism   **D** predation

12. The _____ is a system of production, distribution, and consumption.
    A ecosystem   **B** community   **C** economy   **D** government

Chapter 4 Vocabulary Review, continued

13. A sweet liquid produced by many flowers is known as _____.

     A pollen   **B** serum   **C** xylem   **D** nectar

14. A(n) _____ is someone interested in preserving species and ecosystems.

     A conservationist   **B** naturalist   **C** economist   **D** botanist

15. In the process of _____, better-suited organisms survive to pass on their genes.

     A predation   **C** taxonomy

     B symbiosis   **D** natural selection

16. An organism that provides food for a parasite is called a _____.

     A prey   **B** host   **C** predator   **D** specimen

Directions Match the items in Column A with those in Column B. Write the letter of each correct answer on the line.

Column A	Column B
_____ **17.** inside a city	**A** ecosystem service
_____ **18.** to breed together	**B** extinction
_____ **19.** a quick study of an area's biological diversity	**C** interbreed
_____ **20.** the complete loss of all members of a species	**D** rapid assessment
_____ **21.** a benefit provided by Earth's ecosystems	**E** urban
_____ **22.** the process of genetic change over time	**F** adaptation
_____ **23.** a trait that makes an organism better suited to its environment	**G** evolution
_____ **24.** tiny particles that help fertilize plants	**H** pollen
_____ **25.** the diversity of species on Earth	**I** species diversity
_____ **26.** having to do with religion or the soul	**J** spiritual

Chapter 4 Vocabulary Review, continued

Column A	**Column B**

Column A

_____ **27.** a basic part of many people's diets

_____ **28.** carries information about traits that is passed down from parents to offspring

_____ **29.** protecting natural resources

_____ **30.** scattering seeds away from a parent plant

_____ **31.** separate; different

_____ **32.** a soft-bodied animal that lives in a hard shell

_____ **33.** an inherited characteristic

_____ **34.** a period of time when high numbers of species become extinct

_____ **35.** an example of a species

_____ **36.** an organism that contributes to the diversity of an ecosystem

_____ **37.** having to do with money

Column B

K conservation

L distinct

M gene

N seed dispersal

O staple crop

P economic

Q keystone species

R mass extinction

S mollusk

T specimen

U trait

Directions Read each statement. Unscramble the word or words in parentheses to complete each sentence. Write the answer on the line.

38. The transfer of pollen between plants is called _____. (opnilatnoil)

39. A(n) _____ absorbs food from a host and harms it. (tesapair)

40. A(n) _____ is a small part of a larger unit. (pemlas)

41. The diversity of ecosystems on Earth is known as _____. (yetomssec tidevyrsi)

42. A close relationship between two species is called _____. (ossbimiys)

43. A(n) _____ is a sudden change in an organism's genes. (umattoin)

44. Animals that are _____ are at risk of extinction. (neddergaen)

45. A relationship that benefits both species involved is known as _____. (tulamisum)

What Is a Biome?

Directions Write the letter of the answer that best completes each sentence.

1. Scientists group ecosystems into larger areas called _____.

   A habitats   **B** categories   **C** communities   **D** biomes

2. _____ gives the distance north or south of the equator.

   A Longitude   **B** Altitude   **C** Latitude   **D** Salinity

3. Organisms that live or grow in water are _____.

   A aquatic   **C** seasonal

   B local   **D** terrestrial

4. _____ is how high a place is above sea level.

   A Latitude   **B** Altitude   **C** Longitude   **D** Salinity

5. _____ biomes contain more salt than other aquatic biomes.

   A Saltwater   **B** Freshwater   **C** Terrestrial   **D** River

6. The amount of salt contained in a sample of water is called its _____.

   A altitude   **B** salinity   **C** region   **D** category

Directions Answer each question on the line. Use complete sentences.

7. What are Earth's 10 major terrestrial biomes?

_____

_____

8. What characterizes the terrestrial biomes?

_____

9. How are ecosystems grouped into terrestrial biomes?

_____

_____

10. How are aquatic biomes grouped?

_____

_____

Rain Forest Biomes

Directions Match the items in Column A with those in Column B.
Write the letter of each correct answer on the line.

Column A

_____ **1.** removal of forests for land development

_____ **2.** the part of a forest below the canopy

_____ **3.** native to a place

_____ **4.** to harvest trees and use their wood

_____ **5.** the "roof" of the rain forest

_____ **6.** decomposing material fallen to the ground

_____ **7.** special root structures that help support giant trees

_____ **8.** trees that stick up through the canopy

Column B

A buttress

B canopy

C emergents

D deforestation

E forest floor

F indigenous

G log

H understory

Directions When you compare and contrast, you tell how things
are alike and how they are different. Compare and contrast
the pairs of words below.

9. tropical rain forests and temperate rain forests

   A How they are alike: _____

_____

   B How they are different: _____

_____

10. understory and forest floor

   A How they are alike: _____

_____

   B How they are different: _____

_____

Deciduous and Coniferous Biomes

Directions Choose the term from the Word Bank that completes each sentence correctly. Write the answer on the line.

Word Bank		
acidic	dormant	reptile
amphibian	evergreen	taiga
conifer	hibernate	temperate
coniferous forests	humus	deciduous forests
coniferous trees	latitude	
deciduous trees	migrate	

1. An egg-laying animal that breathes with lungs is a(n) _____.

2. A(n) _____ is a tree that produces its seeds in cones.

3. Some trees become _____, or inactive, in the winter.

4. Coniferous forests are also called the _____.

5. Decomposed plant and animal material called _____ is part of fertile soil.

6. Needles that fall on the soil in coniferous forests make the soil _____.

7. A(n) _____ is an animal that spends part of its life in the water and part on land.

8. Many animals _____, or move from one region, climate, or environment to another.

9. Some animals _____ in a sleeplike condition to pass the winter.

10. Another name for a coniferous tree is _____.

11. The temperate deciduous forests are found between 30° and 50° north _____.

12. Instead of leaves, _____ have needles.

13. Every autumn, _____ shed their leaves.

14. The eastern half of North America is covered mostly by _____.

15. The _____ make up the largest terrestrial biome in the world.

Grassland Biomes

Directions Use the terms in the Word Bank to complete
the paragraph. Write the terms on the lines.

Word Bank		
Antarctica	grass	prairies
diversity	grassland	savannas

The **1.** _____ biomes get less precipitation than

forest biomes. Biomes that receive little rain have less animal

2. _____ than those that get a lot of rain. Grasslands

are found on every continent except **3.** _____. Some

grasslands are mostly **4.** _____. Others have small shrubs mixed with

other dry-weather plants. Tropical grasslands are **5.** _____.

They contain scattered trees. Temperate grasslands are called

6. _____. In these regions, the soil is very rich.

Directions Unscramble the word in parentheses to complete each sentence.
Write the answer on the line.

7. The top, fertile layer of soil is called _____. (spooilt)

8. During _____, farm animals eat more of the native
vegetation than is healthy for the soil. (greozavrgni)

9. Dry grasslands called _____ have short scrubby
plants and are found in coastal areas. (plahaarrc)

10. Most plants in the grasslands have small, hard leaves that
_____, or save, water. (eecvorns)

Tundra and Desert Biomes

Directions Choose the term from the Word Bank that completes each sentence correctly. Write the answer on the line.

Word Bank		
alpine	cold	hot
Arctic	deserts	permafrost
bog	extract	tundra

1. Oil companies remove, or _____, oil and minerals from the soil.

2. Permanently frozen soil found in the tundra is called _____.

3. The _____ biomes are treeless plains that stay frozen for most of the year.

4. A(n) _____ is an area of wet, spongy ground full of decomposing plant matter.

5. Hot biomes that get less than 25 cm of precipitation a year are called _____.

6. In a(n) _____ desert, temperatures are high all year.

7. The tundra located north of the Arctic Circle is called the _____ tundra.

8. A desert where temperatures can drop below 0°C is a _____ desert.

9. The _____ tundra is located above the tree line of high mountains.

Directions Write the letter *A* if the description is for alpine tundra. Write *B* for arctic tundra. Write *AB* if the description is for both.

_____ **10.** short growing season, desertlike conditions

_____ **11.** located north of the Arctic Circle

_____ **12.** found on the tops of mountains

_____ **13.** tundra habitat with longer growing season

_____ **14.** has carnivores like foxes and polar bears

_____ **15.** extremely cold region where soil is permanently frozen

Marine Biomes

Directions Choose the term from the Word Bank that completes each sentence correctly. Write the answer on the line.

Word Bank

abyss	intertidal zone	nursery
aphotic	krill	oceanic zone
coral	mangrove	photic
disphotic zone	marine biomes	phytoplankton
estuary	neritic zone	vertical zone

1. The _____ is the deepest ocean zone.

2. Aquatic biomes that contain large amounts of salt are called _____.

3. Tiny shrimplike animals called _____ provide food for other marine animals.

4. The _____ is the middle ocean depth with little to no light.

5. The _____ is between high and low tide marks.

6. An ocean zone classified by water depth is a(n) _____.

7. The open ocean is also called the _____.

8. The zone between the intertidal zone and the edge of the continental shelf is known as the _____.

9. A(n) _____ is a marine ecosystem where freshwater and salt water meet.

10. A place where marine organisms hatch and grow is called a(n) _____.

11. Coastal wetlands include salt marshes and _____ swamps.

12. In salt water, colonies of tiny polyps form _____ reefs.

13. The topmost level of the ocean is the _____ zone.

14. The base of many marine food chains is made of _____.

15. In the _____ zone of the ocean, the water is cold and dark.

Freshwater Biomes

Directions Use the clue to complete the word below it.

1. An inland body of freshwater shallow enough for plants to grow is a _____.

p		n	d

2. A _____ is the bed of a river or stream that directs flowing water.

c	h		n	n		l

3. A _____ is an inland body of freshwater mostly too deep for plants to grow in.

l		k	

4. Soils saturated with water are referred to as being _____.

w		t		r	l		g	g		d

5. Water is a _____ resource, which means it can run out.

f		n		t	

6. The _____ is the upper part of a river or stream near its source.

h			d	w		t		r	s

7. The place where a river enters a larger body of water is its _____.

m			t	h

8. Some ponds are _____. They dry up during part of the year.

s			s		n		l

9. To create by physical processes is to _____.

g		n		r		t	

10. Streams and rivers are examples of _____ water.

f	l		w		n	g

Chapter 5 Vocabulary Review

Directions Chose the term from the Word Bank that completes each sentence correctly. Write the answer on the line.

Word Bank		
acidic	deforestation	latitude
conifer	extract	wetland
deciduous tree	intertidal zone	

1. The _____ is the zone between high and low tide marks.

2. When forests are removed in order to develop land, it is called _____.

3. The distance north or south of the equator is known as _____.

4. A(n) _____ sheds its leaves at the end of the growing season.

5. Soil containing high levels of acid is called _____.

6. To _____ is to take out or harvest.

7. A(n) _____ is a cone-bearing tree with needles that stays green year-round.

8. A low area that is saturated with water is known as a(n) _____.

Word Bank		
bog	hibernate	tundra
emergent	marine biome	vertical zone
finite	savannas	

9. The _____ biome is a frozen treeless plain that receives very little precipitation.

10. A tree that grows taller than the rain forest canopy is known as a(n)_____.

11. Some animals _____, or become inactive during the winter.

12. An ocean zone classified by water depth is called a(n) _____.

13. Tropical grasslands called _____ contain scattered trees and are found near the equator.

▶ Environmental Science

Chapter 5 Vocabulary Review, continued

14. A saltwater ecosystem is known as a(n) _____.

15. A(n) _____ is an area of wet, spongy ground full of decomposing plant matter.

16. A resource that is limited and can run out is called _____.

Word Bank		
amphibian	mouth	salinity
chaparral	nursery	topsoil
desert	oceanic zone	understory

17. The _____ of seawater describes the amount of salt dissolved in it.

18. An animal that spends part of its life in water and part on land is called a(n) _____.

19. The forest layer beneath the canopy is called the _____.

20. The _____ of a river or stream is where it enters another, larger body of water.

21. Marine organisms hatch and grow in a(n) _____.

22. The _____ is a dry grassland found in coastal regions.

23. A hot area that receives less than 25 cm of precipitation a year is known as a(n) _____.

24. The top, fertile layer of soil is known as _____.

25. The _____ is the open ocean.

Directions Define each term.

26. terrestrial _____

27. aquatic _____

28. altitude _____

29. canopy _____

30. indigenous _____

Chapter 5 Vocabulary Review, continued

31. migrate _____

32. dormant _____

33. evergreen _____

34. conserve _____

35. krill _____

36. detritus _____

37. colony _____

38. saturated _____

39. estuary _____

40. waterlogged _____

Directions Match the items in Column A with those in Column B.
Write the letter of each correct answer on the line.

Column A

_____ **41.** inland body of freshwater too deep for
plants to grow on the bottom

_____ **42.** forest in tropical regions that receives a large
amount of rain

_____ **43.** tundra located above the tree line on high mountains

_____ **44.** to harvest trees and use their wood

_____ **45.** temperate grasslands with very fertile soil

Column B

A alpine tundra

B lake

C log

D prairies

E tropical rain forest

Chapter 5 Vocabulary Review, continued

Column A

_____ **46.** group of ecosystems with similar temperatures and rainfall, or salinity and water depth

_____ **47.** forest in temperate regions that receives a large amount of rain

_____ **48.** a microscopic plant that forms the base of the marine food chain

_____ **49.** water with high amounts of dissolved salt

_____ **50.** large, open, grassy biome with few shrubs and trees

_____ **51.** another name for prairie

_____ **52.** water with low amounts of dissolved salt

_____ **53.** microscopic animals that float freely in water

_____ **54.** permanently frozen ground at high latitudes or high altitudes

_____ **55.** the deepest ocean zone

_____ **56.** also known as taiga

_____ **57.** layer of decomposing material that covers the soil in a forest

_____ **58.** tundra located north of the Arctic Circle

_____ **59.** special root structures that support a tree

_____ **60.** marine ecosystem formed from the skeletons of corals

Column B

F biome

G grassland

H phytoplankton

I salt water

J temperate rain forest

K abyss

L freshwater

M permafrost

N temperate grassland

O zooplankton

P Arctic tundra

Q buttress

R coniferous forest

S coral reef

T forest floor

Chapter 5 Vocabulary Review, continued

Column A	**Column B**

Column A

_____ **61.** forest in temperate regions where trees shed their leaves in the winter

_____ **62.** to create by physical process

_____ **63.** inland body of freshwater shallow enough for plants to grow on the bottom

_____ **64.** zone between the intertidal zone and the edge of the continental shelf

_____ **65.** the plant life found in an area

Column B

U generate

V pond

W neritic zone

X temperate deciduous forest

Y vegetation

Directions Write the letter of the answer that best completes each sentence.

66. The _____ are parts of a river or stream near their sources.

   A headwaters   **B** channels   **C** mouths   **D** estuaries

67. The zone of ocean life where there is no light is called the _____.

   A neritic zone   **B** aphotic zone   **C** disphotic zone   **D** photic zone

68. Bodies of freshwater that have no flowing water are known as _____.

   A coastal wetlands   **C** standing-water ecosystems

   B intertidal zones   **D** flowing-water ecosystems

69. A long coral reef that protects the shore from winds and tides is called a(n) _____.

   A barrier reef   **B** atoll   **C** fringe reef   **D** island reef

70. Things that are _____ only exist during certain times of the year.

   A temperate   **B** yearly   **C** aphotic   **D** seasonal

71. A _____ is an area that receives very little rainfall and is hot all year.

   A tundra   **B** hot desert   **C** cold desert   **D** temperate deciduous forest

72. Decomposed plant and animal material make up a rich layer of soil called _____.

   A topsoil   **B** humus   **C** permafrost   **D** bedrock

Chapter 5 Vocabulary Review, continued

73. A marsh that is periodically flooded by marine water is called a(n) _____.

   A barrier reef   **B** estuary   **C** salt marsh   **D** bog

74. A(n) _____ is a scaly, egg-laying animal that breathes using lungs.

   A reptile   **B** amphibian   **C** bony fish   **D** mammal

75. The bed of a river or stream that directs flowing water is known as a(n) _____.

   A headwater   **B** channel   **C** mouth   **D** estuary

76. The _____ is the top zone of the ocean that gets sunlight all year.

   A abyss   **B** aphotic zone   **C** neritic zone   **D** photic zone

77. A freshwater ecosystem with moving water is called a(n) _____.

   A standing-water ecosystem   **C** salt marsh
   B flowing-water ecosystem   **D** estuary

78. A(n) _____ is covered by salt water or is washed by tides daily.

   A coral reef   **B** channel   **C** coastal wetland   **D** swamp

79. When _____ occurs, animals eat more vegetation than is healthy for the soil.

   A herding   **B** deforestation   **C** logging   **D** overgrazing

80. A very dry region where temperatures can drop to 0°C is called a _____.

   A cold desert   **B** savanna   **C** hot desert   **D** taiga

81. The middle zone of ocean life that gets little or no light is called the _____.

   A intertidal zone   **B** aphotic zone   **C** disphotic zone   **D** photic zone

82. Saltwater swamps dominated by mangrove trees are known as _____.

   A lakes   **B** ponds   **C** mangrove swamps   **D** bogs

83. Another name for coniferous forest is _____.

   A chapparral   **B** savanna   **C** taiga   **D** wetland

84. A(n) _____ is determined by distance from the shore.

   A horizontal zone   **C** aphotic zone
   B photic zone   **D** vertical zone

A Growing Population

Directions Match the items in Column A with those in Column B.
Write the letter of each correct answer on the line.

Column A

1. At the current rate of growth, nearly _____ will be added to the world today.

2. Usually, growth rate is expressed _____.

3. Today, the total number of people on Earth is more than _____.

4. One reason humans greatly impact the environment is because their _____.

5. By 2050, the population could be more than _____.

6. Exponential growth means the population grows by _____.

Column B

A population is large

B 6.4 billion

C 9 billion

D as a percent

E larger amounts each year

F 233,000 people

Directions Choose the term from the Word Bank that completes each sentence correctly. Write the answer on the line.

Word Bank	
growth rate	migration
J-curve	world population

7. On a graph, exponential growth forms a _____.

8. The number of people added to or subtracted from a population each year is the _____.

9. The total number of people on the earth, the _____, increases each year.

10. A large movement of people or animals from one place to another is a _____.

Population Patterns

Directions Write the letter of the answer that best completes each sentence.

1. Populations that stay the same size are _____.

   A overpopulated   **B** underpopulated   **C** stabilized   **D** changing

2. In _____, the population is too large to be supported by the resources available.

   A overpopulation   **C** growth

   B conservation   **D** family planning

3. A change in population over time is called a _____.

   A stabilizing effect   **C** developing nation

   B population trend   **D** poverty level

4. _____ have strong economies based on manufacturing and technology.

   A Developing nations   **C** Industrialized nations

   B Subsistence agriculture   **D** Demographers

5. People who study populations are called _____.

   A paleontologists   **B** botanists   **C** demographers   **D** chemists

6. Females reach their _____ when they are old enough to begin having children.

   A trends   **C** life expectancy

   B poverty level   **D** reproductive age

Directions Match the items in Column A with those in Column B. Write the letter of each correct answer on the line.

	Column A		Column B
_____	**7.** the average number of births per woman	**A**	family planning
_____	**8.** deciding when and how many children to have	**B**	fertility rate
_____	**9.** the total number of years a person is expected to live	**C**	life expectancy
_____	**10.** disposal of waste	**D**	sanitation

Consumption and the Environment

Directions Choose the term from the Word Bank that completes each sentence correctly. Write the answer on the line.

Word Bank		
consumption	fossil fuels	renewable
fisheries	mining	toxic waste

1. A _____ material is poisonous to the environment.

2. Industries that catch and sell fish are _____.

3. Using resources and creating waste is called _____.

4. Sources of energy from fossilized plants and animals are _____.

5. In _____, minerals are extracted from the earth.

6. Some resources are _____, or able to be replaced by natural processes.

Directions Answer each question on the lines. Use complete sentences.

7. Name two factors that affect the rate of consumption.

_____

_____

8. Why is consumption important for people?

_____

_____

9. What are three negative impacts of consumption?

_____

_____

_____

10. In what countries are consumption rates the highest?

_____

_____

Balancing Needs

Directions Unscramble the word in parentheses to complete each sentence. Write the answer on the line.

1. A person's wealth is referred to as _____. (enefuflac)

2. Another word for fairness is _____. (yqtuie)

3. Goods that are not harmful to the environment are _____. (tcioxnno)

4. People suffering from _____ do not get the nutrients they need to keep them healthy. (nnttlamuiroi)

5. Decayed organic matter used to add nutrients to the soil is _____. (tcpooms)

6. People who are significantly overweight suffer from _____. (bytiseo)

Directions Answer each question on the lines. Use complete sentences.

7. Why do experts believe the impact of consumption will get worse?

_____

_____

8. How are people changing their consumption habits?

_____

_____

9. How are manufacturers changing their consumption habits?

_____

_____

10. Explain the sustainable harvest of wood.

_____

_____

Chapter 6 Vocabulary Review

Directions Write the word or words that complete each sentence correctly. Find the word in the puzzle. Words may be forward, backward, upside down, or diagonal.

1. Another word for wealth is _____.

2. A(n) _____ is a large movement of people from one place to another.

3. To _____ is to remain the same.

4. When someone dies because of hunger, they _____.

5. A(n) population _____ is a change in population over time.

6. Another word for fairness is _____.

7. The disposal of waste is known as _____.

8. To _____ is to extract minerals from the earth.

9. Industries that catch and sell fish are known as _____.

N	O	I	T	A	T	I	N	A	S
E	O	P	W	C	C	C	E	E	E
E	N	I	M	F	U	S	I	Q	Z
F	B	I	T	V	T	R	W	U	I
H	W	V	M	A	E	H	Z	I	L
A	X	V	R	H	R	R	Q	T	I
A	V	V	S	M	O	G	T	Y	B
O	E	I	S	P	E	A	I	Y	A
P	F	D	N	E	R	T	O	M	T
A	F	F	L	U	E	N	C	E	S

Chapter 6 Vocabulary Review, continued

Directions Match the items in Column A with those in Column B.
Write the letter of each correct answer on the line.

Column A

_____ **10.** usual way of life for a person, community, or country

_____ **11.** harvested in a way that does not damage an ecosystem

_____ **12.** when a population is too large to be supported
by local resources

_____ **13.** the total number of years a person is expected to live

_____ **14.** not poisonous to the environment

_____ **15.** total number of people on Earth

_____ **16.** the largest number of living things an area can support

_____ **17.** energy sources like oil or coal that came from
fossilized plants and animals

_____ **18.** waste that can be poisonous to living things

_____ **19.** design that reduces the impact of production

_____ **20.** a curve showing exponential growth

_____ **21.** deciding when to have children and how
many children to have

_____ **22.** a nation with well-developed industries and economies

_____ **23.** the rate at which a population is increasing or decreasing

_____ **24.** the process of using resources and producing waste

_____ **25.** not getting enough calories or nutrients from food

_____ **26.** the number of births per 1,000 people in a given year

_____ **27.** growing just enough food to support immediate
local needs

Column B

A life expectancy

B nontoxic

C overpopulation

D standard of living

E sustainably harvested

F world population

G carrying capacity

H environmentally
intelligent design

I family planning

J fossil fuels

K J-curve

L toxic waste

M birth rate

N consumption

O industrialized nation

P growth rate

Q malnutrition

R subsistence agriculture

Chapter 6 Vocabulary Review, continued

Directions Unscramble the word or words in parentheses to complete each sentence. Write the answer on the line.

28. A person of _____ is neither too old nor too young to have children. (doructeervip gea)

29. The state of being significantly overweight is called _____. (yisebot)

30. A resource that is _____ can be renewed by natural processes. (waneerleb)

31. A(n) _____ is a nation that has not yet become industrialized. (pogevlendi tonnia)

32. Growth that increases by a larger and larger amount is called _____. (peatlixnneo wotghr)

33. The average number of births per woman is known as the _____. (yitetrilf tera)

34. A _____ is a scientist who studies populations. (gopedmarhre)

35. Decomposed organic waste that is high in nutrients is called _____. (toompsc)

36. The _____ is the number of deaths per 1,000 people in a given year. (tadhe erta)

37. The amount one must earn to afford the things needed to live is called the _____. (vortyep eellv)

Energy Basics

Directions Choose the term from the Word Bank that completes each sentence correctly. Write the answer on the line.

Word Bank

first law of energy	nonrenewable	transport
kinetic energy	second law of energy	utility
inefficient	transform	vibrations
law		

---

1. The _____ states that energy changes from high-quality to low-quality forms.

2. A principle is also called a(n)_____.

3. A dropped rock releases its energy as _____ into the ground.

4. To _____ is to change from one form to another.

5. The _____ states that energy is neither created nor destroyed.

6. A car burning gasoline is wasteful, or _____.

7. A(n) _____ is a company that provides a public service, such as water or electricity.

8. Energy is not always easy to _____, or move from one place to another.

9. Resources that are only available in a limited supply are _____.

10. The energy in a moving car is _____.

Fossil Fuels

Directions Write the letter of the answer that best completes each sentence.

1. A _____ converts, or changes, crude oil into gasoline or heating oil.

   A dam   **B** generator   **C** turbine   **D** refinery

2. A machine that generates electricity is called a _____.

   A refinery   **B** generator   **C** turbine   **D** diatom

3. Most fossil fuels come from tiny, ancient algae called _____.

   A diatoms   **B** turbines   **C** reserves   **D** coal

4. _____ is another name for crude oil.

   A Coal   **B** Petroleum   **C** Contaminate   **D** Refinery

5. _____ is a thick, liquid mixture of hydrogen, carbon, and other elements.

   A Methane   **B** Sulfur oxide   **C** Crude oil   **D** Coal

6. _____ are places where a certain amount of oil is known to be available.

   A Reserves   **B** Refineries   **C** Generators   **D** Power plants

Directions Choose the term from the Word Bank that completes each question correctly. Write the answer on the line.

7. Natural gas can be used for fuel after its _____ are removed.

8. Decomposing plant material that was under pressure for millions of years formed _____.

9. In the process of _____, the top layer of plants, soil, and rock are removed to expose the layers of coal.

10. In _____, large "rooms" are carved out of coal deposits.

Word Bank
coal
impurities
strip mining
tunnel mining

Nuclear Energy

Directions Use the terms in the Word Bank to complete the paragraph. Write the terms on the lines.

Word Bank	
chain reaction	nuclear reactor
nuclear fission	radioactive
nuclear power plant	uranium

A process called **1.** _____ releases energy trapped inside

an atom. The process releases neutrons inside atoms. These neutrons split

other atoms. This starts a **2.** _____ that produces a lot of

energy. The elements used in nuclear reactions are isotopes that are

3. _____. One type of radioactive isotope is

4. _____. Nuclear reactions take place inside of a

5. _____. The energy from these reactions is then

converted to electricity in a **6.** _____.

Directions Choose the term from the Word Bank that completes each sentence correctly. Write the answer on the line.

Word Bank	
leukemia	uranium mills
tailings	ventilation

7. A disease of the blood that may be caused by radiation

is _____.

8. Uranium is dug out of the ground then processed in _____.

9. People working in mines rely on _____ to supply

fresh air.

10. Radioactive mines and mills produce waste called _____.

Solar Energy

Directions Match the items in Column A with those in Column B. Write the letter of each correct answer on the line.

Column A

_____ **1.** uses dense building materials

_____ **2.** keeps sunlight and heated air away from a building

_____ **3.** the most basic form of solar energy

Column B

A passive solar cooling

B passive solar energy

C passive solar heating

Directions Use the clue to complete the word below it.

4. The process of _____ uses sunlight to replace or supplement artificial light.

d			l		g	h	t		n	g

5. Energy from the sun is called _____ energy.

s		l		r

6. Any material that prevents heat or cold from passing in or out is _____.

	n	s		l		t			n

7. In _____ solar systems, the sun's energy is absorbed with solar collectors.

	c	t		v	

8. A solar _____ converts the sun's energy into heat.

c		l	l		c	t		r

9. Devices that convert sunlight into electricity are _____.

p	h		t		v		l	t			c	s

10. An electrical _____ is used to distribute electricity to a region.

p		w		r		g	r		d

Energy from Earth's Natural Systems

Directions Unscramble the word in parentheses to complete each sentence. Write the answer on the line.

1. Power produced by moving water is called _____.
(rwoeorphyd)

2. Barriers built across rivers are _____. (asmd)

3. To move _____ means to travel against the flow of the water in a river or stream. (mpurtsae)

4. Fish _____ are sometimes used to help fish travel upstream. (sladerd)

5. To move _____ means to travel in the same direction as the water. (nsowmreatd)

6. The gravity of the sun and moon cause _____, which affect the surface of the ocean. (dseit)

7. A wind _____ converts wind movement into energy. (bneirut)

8. Designers of power systems must keep _____, or visual appearance, in mind. (tseathecsi)

9. A group of wind turbines form a wind _____. (mfra)

10. A hot _____ is a natural flow of groundwater heated inside the earth. (gpnsir)

Directions Choose the term from the Word Bank that completes each sentence correctly. Write the answer on the line.

11. A spongelike, brown material is _____.
It is made of partly decomposed plants.

12. Heat from inside the earth is referred to as _____.

13. A(n) _____ is a jet of hot liquid or steam shooting out of Earth's crust.

14. Organic material made by plants and animals is _____.

15. A type of fuel made from corn or sugar is _____.

Word Bank
biomass
ethanol
geothermal
geyser
peat

Energy for the Future

Directions Choose the term from the Word Bank that completes each sentence correctly. Write the answer on the line.

Word Bank		
compact fluorescent	energy efficient	hybrid vehicle
consumer	fuel cell	mandated

1. A(n) _____ runs on both a gasoline engine and an electric motor.

2. One type of energy-efficient lightbulb is the _____ lightbulb.

3. Products that do not waste energy are described as _____.

4. A person who buys and uses products is a _____.

5. Sometimes energy conservation is _____, or enforced by law.

6. A(n) _____ is a device that converts substances like hydrogen and oxygen to electricity.

Directions Answer each question on the lines.

7. Why will the demand for fossil fuel have to change in the future?

_____

8. What are two simple things people can do to conserve energy?

_____

9. How much oil could be saved if home temperatures were lowered by six degrees?

_____

10. Between 1970 and 1985, why did cars become more energy efficient?

_____

Chapter 7 Vocabulary Review

Directions Choose the term from the Word Bank that completes each sentence correctly. Write the answer on the line.

Word Bank		
downstream	meltdown	turbine
ethanol	passive solar cooling	utility
first law of energy	refinery	
isotopes	second law of energy	

1. When the core of a nuclear reactor completely melts, it is known as a(n) _____.

2. Corn and sugar cane can be used to make _____, which is a liquid fuel.

3. Crude oil is turned into usable forms of energy in a _____.

4. The _____ states that energy is neither created nor destroyed.

5. Atoms of the same element with different numbers of neutrons are called _____.

6. A(n) _____ is a device with spinning blades that is used to create electricity.

7. Organisms swimming _____ are moving with the flow of water.

8. A company that performs a public service is called a(n) _____.

9. The _____ states that energy always changes from high-quality to low-quality forms.

10. Cooling a building by blocking sunlight from it is an example of _____.

Chapter 7 Vocabulary Review, continued

Directions Choose the term from the Word Bank that completes each sentence correctly. Write the answer on the line.

Word Bank		
carpool	passive solar heating	upstream
core	peat	wind farm
natural gas	sulfur oxide	
nuclear power plant	tide	

11. A fuel known as _____ is a combination of several gases, mostly methane.

12. When people _____, they share rides with others to reduce energy use.

13. A(n) _____ is the regular rise and fall of the ocean's surface.

14. Partly decomposed plant material found in wetlands is called _____.

15. The center of a nuclear reactor is known as the _____.

16. A(n) _____ is a facility where nuclear energy is converted to electricity.

17. One of the air pollutants produced by burning fossil fuels is _____.

18. A(n) _____ contains many connected groups of wind turbines.

19. If an organism swims _____, it is moving against the flow of the water.

20. When a building is heated directly by sunlight, it is called _____.

Chapter 7 Vocabulary Review, continued

Directions Use the terms in the Word Bank to complete
the paragraph. Write the terms on the lines.

Word Bank	
electrons	protons
neutrons	subatomic particles
nucleus	

Atoms are made up of three smaller particles called **21.** _____.

The center of an atom contains positively charged **22.** _____

and **23.** _____ that have no charge. These

two types of particles make up the core, or **24.** _____

of the atom. The atom's core is surrounded by negatively charged

particles called **25.** _____.

Word Bank	
coal	strip mining
deposits	tunnel mining
mountaintop removal	

A solid fossil fuel called **26.** _____ is made of almost

pure carbon. It comes from decomposed plants that were under pressure

for millions of years. This fossil fuel is found in underground layers,

called **27.** _____, between layers of rock. There are

several ways to collect this material. In **28.** _____,

the surface layer of rock is removed and the fuel is taken out. Another

form of extraction is **29.** _____, or pit mining.

A third type of mining is **30.** _____, where the

entire top of a mountain is removed with dynamite.

Chapter 7 Vocabulary Review, continued

Directions Read each statement. Circle the answer that correctly completes each sentence.

31. A (turbine, fuel cell, utility) is a device for converting chemicals
to electricity.

32. The percentage of useful work from a certain amount of energy is (power
usage, conservation, energy efficiency).

33. When sunlight is used to replace artificial light, it is known as
(photovoltaics, solar collectors, daylighting).

34. A (radioactive, passive, hybrid) element gives off energy while it is changing
into another substance.

35. Naturally flowing water that is heated inside the earth is called a (geyser,
tide, hot spring).

36. A gas called (methane, crude oil, sulfur oxide) is released by
decaying organisms.

37. Energy produced directly by sunlight with no extra machinery is called
(hydroelectricity, passive solar energy, active solar systems).

38. To (transport, vibrate, transform) is to change from one form to another.

39. A thick liquid fossil fuel called (crude oil, methane, coal) is found in
underground deposits.

40. Fresh air is supplied though (ventilation, tailings, photovoltaics).

41. A (generator, geothermal, chain reaction) is a reaction that causes
itself to continue.

42. Burning fossil fuels can release a pollutant called (petroleum, natural gas,
nitrogen oxide).

43. The energy of motion is called (kinetic energy, potential energy,
solar energy).

44. Devices called (fuel cells, active solar systems, turbines) collect and deliver
solar energy.

45. Plant material that is burned for fuel is known as (tailings, biomass,
natural gas).

46. Uranium is processed in a (fuel cell, nuclear power plant, uranium mill).

47. A machine that generates electricity is called a (uranium mill, nuclear
reactor, generator).

Chapter 7 Vocabulary Review, continued

48. Tiny algae called (neutrons, diatoms, deposits) were found in the ocean millions of years ago.

49. Nuclear fission takes place in a (turbine, nuclear reactor, strip mine).

50. The process of producing energy by splitting atoms is called (radioactive decay, nuclear fission, kinetic energy).

51. Material that prevents heat or cold from escaping into or out of a space is called (petroleum, peat, insulation).

52. Resources that are (nonrenewable, renewable, recycled) are only available in limited supply.

53. Barriers built across a river to control the flow of water are called (dams, fish ladders, control rods).

54. A (hybrid vehicle, wind turbine, generator) runs on gasoline and an electric motor.

55. Nonradioactive rods used to control nuclear fission are called (cores, control rods, fuel rods).

Directions Match the items in Column A with those in Column B.
Write the letter of each correct answer on the line.

Column A	Column B
_____ **56.** to move from one place to another	**A** aesthetics
_____ **57.** movement back and forth	**B** fish ladder
_____ **58.** series of pools that allow fish to move upstream over a dam	**C** geyser
	D transport
_____ **59.** jet of hot liquid or steam that shoots out of a crack in Earth's crust	**E** vibration
_____ **60.** visual appearance	

Chapter 7 Vocabulary Review, continued

Column A

_____ **61.** wasteful

_____ **62.** a principle

_____ **63.** heat from inside the earth

_____ **64.** tower with moving blades that converts wind movement to energy

_____ **65.** thick liquid fossil fuel found underground; crude oil

_____ **66.** energy stored in an object

_____ **67.** energy from moving water

_____ **68.** energy from the sun

_____ **69.** pollution or contamination

_____ **70.** enforced by law

_____ **71.** radioactive element used in nuclear fission

_____ **72.** device that captures solar energy and converts it to heat

_____ **73.** energy-efficient lightbulbs

_____ **74.** using and wasting less energy

_____ **75.** solar cells; convert solar energy to electricity

Column B

F geothermal

G inefficient

H law

I petroleum

J wind turbine

K hydropower

L impurity

M mandated

N potential energy

O solar energy

P compact fluorescents

Q energy conservation

R photovoltaics

S solar collector

T uranium

Directions Unscramble the word or words in parentheses to complete each sentence. Write the letter on the line.

76. A(n) _____ is the amount of a natural resource known to be available. (verseer)

77. When something is _____, it wastes less energy. (neyreg ficetenif)

Chapter 7 Vocabulary Review, continued

78. Debris produced by mining is called _____. (glisnait)

79. A(n) _____ is a network of power lines that distributes energy to a region. (werpo digr)

80. A(n) _____ is a radioactive rod used in nuclear fission. (lefu odr)

81. Cancer of the blood cells is called _____. (ealkumei)

82. To pollute an area is to _____ it. (tamicontena)

Global Water Resources

Directions Choose the term from the Word Bank that completes each sentence correctly. Write the answer on the line.

Word Bank			
aquifer	recharge zone	recreation	seeps
depleted	recharge	scarcity	well

1. Underground layers of rock, sand, or gravel that trap water make a(n) _____.

2. The _____ is an area that allows water to refill an aquifer.

3. People can access groundwater by digging a deep hole called a(n) _____.

4. Groundwater starts with rain or snow that _____, or soaks, into the ground.

5. Water from rain, snow, and streams helps _____ an aquifer.

6. Surface water is often used for _____, like swimming, boating, or fishing.

7. Lack, or _____, of water is a huge problem in many parts of the world.

8. Overuse of water from aquifers can cause them to become _____.

Directions When you compare and contrast, you tell how things are alike and how they are different. Compare and contrast the pairs of words below.

9. aquifer and well   **A** How they are alike: _____

_____

B How they are different: _____

_____

10. watershed and water table   **A** How they are alike: _____

_____

B How they are different: _____

_____

Using and Managing Water Resources

Directions Choose the term from the Word Bank that completes each sentence correctly. Write the answer on the line.

Word Bank		
diverted	irrigate	reservoir
drought	landscaping	
industry	purification	

1. Cleaning by separating out pollutants or impurities is called _____.

2. Farmers may _____ their crops using artificially supplied water.

3. The course of a river can be _____ to irrigate crops.

4. During a _____ there is very little rainfall.

5. A(n) _____ is a company that makes or sells particular goods or services.

6. The natural beauty of a piece of land can be improved through _____.

7. A(n) _____ is a natural or artificial lake or pond used for water storage.

Directions Answer each question on the lines. Use complete sentences.

8. What is a sprinkler system?

   _____

   _____

9. Why is a sprinkler system a type of irrigation?

   _____

   _____

10. How does water treatment make water safe for drinking?

    _____

    _____

Water Pollution and Treatment

Directions Choose the term from the Word Bank that completes each sentence correctly. Write the answer on the line.

Word Bank		
eutrophication	organic waste	sewage treatment
fertilizers	runoff	plant
herbicides	sewage	

1. In _____, too many nutrients cause excessive algae growth.

2. Human wastewater called _____ is a source of pollution.

3. Farmers supplement plants with organic and inorganic nutrients called _____.

4. Chemicals that kill weeds are _____.

5. Sewage is cleaned in a _____ before being released.

6. Wastes from living organisms are called _____.

7. Rain or melted snow that washes off of roads and other surfaces is _____.

Directions When you compare and contrast, you tell how things are alike and how they are different. Compare and contrast the pairs of words below.

8. point-source pollution and nonpoint-source pollution

    A How they are alike: _____

    _____

    B How they are different: _____

    _____

9. thermal pollution and radioactive waste

    A How they are alike: _____

    _____

    B How they are different: _____

    _____

10. cholera and hepatitis

    A How they are alike: _____

    _____

    B How they are different: _____

    _____

Protecting Water Resources

Directions Answer each question on the lines. Use complete sentences.

1. How can people preserve water resources for the future?

_____

_____

2. In addition to laws, what else might protect water resources?

_____

_____

3. How can nonnative crops be harmful to the environment?

_____

_____

4. How are industries reducing water use? _____

_____

5. Why does watering the lawn at night help to conserve water?

_____

_____

Directions Unscramble the word or words in parentheses to complete each sentence. Write the answer on the line.

6. Water is delivered in drops directly to the plant's roots using _____. (prid iiirrgnato)

7. A type of landscaping that uses native and drought-tolerant plants is _____. (siignpxacre)

8. Wastewater that does not contain animals waste is called _____. (ryga trawe)

9. Products that are designed to save water are described as _____. (wlo-wlof)

10. To protect water, laws ban the use of deadly _____. (eediespcst)

Chapter 8 Vocabulary Review

Directions Match the items in Column A with those in Column B.
Write the letter of each correct answer on the line.

Column A

_____ **1.** to soak into

_____ **2.** play or amusement

_____ **3.** intestinal infection caused by contaminated water or food

_____ **4.** to turn from one course to another

_____ **5.** waste from living organisms

_____ **6.** heat added to water or air by humans that causes ecological changes

_____ **7.** not allowing water to flow through

_____ **8.** when toxic compounds accumulate through the food chain

_____ **9.** improving the natural beauty of land

_____ **10.** allowing water to flow through

_____ **11.** a disease that damages the liver

_____ **12.** human-generated wastewater

_____ **13.** to use up

_____ **14.** waste contaminated with radioactive materials

_____ **15.** an intestinal infection with severe diarrhea

Column B

A cholera

B divert

C organic waste

D recreation

E seep

F bioaccumulation

G impermeable

H landscaping

I permeable

J thermal pollution

K deplete

L dysentery

M hepatitus

N radioactive waste

O sewage

Chapter 8 Vocabulary Review, continued

Directions Write the letter of the answer that best completes each sentence.

16. Organic and inorganic nutrients that help plants grow are known as _____.

A fertilizers   **B** hormones   **C** herbicides   **D** steroids

17. A pond or lake for the storage of water is known as a _____.

A watershed   **B** reservoir   **C** well   **D** water table

18. A(n) _____ showerhead is designed to use less water.

A fixed   **B** low-flow   **C** irrigation   **D** seep

19. Sewage is cleaned in a(n) _____ before being released into surface water.

A aquifer   **C** sprinkler system

B watershed   **D** sewage treatment plant

20. A(n) _____ is an area underground that contains groundwater.

A well   **B** sinkhole   **C** aquifer   **D** watershed

21. The process of _____ delivers water directly to plant roots.

A drip irrigation   **C** xeriscaping

B root tap   **D** deep irrigation

22. A type of landscaping called _____ uses native and drought-tolerant plants.

A eutrophication   **B** drip irrigation   **C** greenhousing   **D** xeriscaping

23. Water that is visible above the ground is called _____.

A groundwater   **B** surface water   **C** top water   **D** water table

24. A _____ is a nonliving microorganism that can infect cells and cause disease.

A fertilizer   **B** pollutant   **C** bacteria   **D** virus

25. An unusually long period of little rainfall is called a _____.

A low-flow   **B** depletion   **C** drought   **D** flood

26. Chemicals that are used to kill weeds are called _____.

A pesticides   **B** herbicides   **C** organic waste   **D** fertilizer

Chapter 8 Vocabulary Review, continued

27. A(n) _____ is a device that sprays water from above the ground.

    A sprinkler system   **C** water sprayer

    B aquifer   **D** runoff

28. In a _____, water travels downward to become part of an aquifer.

    A recharge zone   **C** reservoir

    B well   **D** sprinkler system

29. Rain or melted snow that flows over land into bodies of water is called _____.

    A groundwater   **C** gray water

    B runoff   **D** surface water

30. Most water goes through _____ to remove harmful chemicals and make it safe to drink.

    A runoff   **C** water treatment

    B eutrophication   **D** drip irrigation

31. A _____ is a hole that is dug or drilled to get water from the earth.

    A sinkhole   **C** well

    B surface water   **D** watershed

32. Wastewater that does not contain animal waste and can be reused is called _____.

    A sewage   **C** runoff

    B organic waste   **D** gray water

33. Viruses and bacteria are examples of _____, which can contaminate water and cause disease.

    A invertebrates   **C** pathogens

    B cells   **D** sewage

Chapter 8 Vocabulary Review, continued

Directions Choose the term from the Word Bank that completes each sentence correctly. Write the answer on the line.

Word Bank	
eutrophication	purification
industry	recharge
irrigate	scarcity
nonpoint-source pollution	water table
point-source pollution	watershed

34. The top of the groundwater layer is known as the _____.

35. Water _____ is cleaning it by separating out pollution and impurities.

36. When _____ occurs, excess nutrients cause excessive plant growth and oxygen depletion.

37. Pollution that comes from a particular source is called _____.

38. Water that seeps into an aquifer will _____, or refill it.

39. In a(n) _____, all the precipitation drains into the same body of water.

40. Many farmers _____ their land to supply their crops with water.

41. A(n) _____ is the making and selling of a particular kind of good or service.

42. Pollution that cannot be traced to a specific source is called _____.

43. When there is a _____, there is a shortage of something that is needed.

Air Pollution and Living Things

Directions Use the terms in the Word Bank to complete the
paragraph. Write the terms on the lines.

Word Bank		
cancer	heart	respiratory
emissions	polluted	vehicles
factories	pollution	

Air pollution affects human health in many ways. It can cause

1. _____ problems and lung **2.** _____.

Asthma and emphysema are two types of **3.** _____, or

breathing, ailments. Both are made worse by breathing **4.** _____

air. More than 600,000 people a year die earlier than they normally would because of

air **5.** _____. To tackle air pollution at the source, experts try to

reduce **6.** _____, or releases of pollutants, from

7. _____, **8.** _____, and other sources.

Directions Read each statement. Circle the answer that
correctly completes each sentence.

9. Bits of solids and liquids in the air are called (droplets, particulate matter, materials).

10. Materials in the air called (particles, chemicals, air pollutants) harm living
things and nonliving materials.

11. Pollution in the air is (air pollution, precipitation, humidity).

12. Pollutants that are released directly into the air by human or natural resources
are (secondary air pollutants, primary air pollutants, particulates).

13. A harmful substance that forms from a reaction between other chemicals in the
air is a (secondary air pollutant, primary air pollutant, precipitation).

14. Pollution that is found and measured in outdoor air is (primary air
pollution, secondary air pollution, outdoor air pollution).

15. Pollution that is found indoors, called (indoor air pollution, primary air
pollution, secondary air pollution), includes items like cleaning products
and insect spray.

Smog, Heat, Noise, and Light

Directions Match the items in Column A with those in Column B.
Write the letter of each correct answer on the line.

Column A

_____ **1.** increased temperatures in areas of human development
and activity

_____ **2.** a harmful gas found in photochemical smog that
can cause headaches and breathing difficulties

_____ **3.** a pollutant associated with industry that is produced
by burning coal and oil

_____ **4.** bothersome brightness or glare caused by
human-made lights

_____ **5.** noise that interrupts daily life

_____ **6.** a device designed to reduce emissions of air pollutants
from vehicle exhaust

Column B

A catalytic converter

B industrial smog

C light pollution

D noise pollution

E ozone

F urban heat island effect

Directions Answer each question on the lines. Use complete sentences.

7. Where is photochemical smog most common?

_____

_____

8. What happens when nitrogen oxides react with sunlight?

_____

_____

9. What are three health problems caused by ozone?

_____

_____

10. What causes the urban heat island effect?

_____

_____

Acid Rain

Directions Complete the science terms by writing the missing letters.
Use the clues to help you.

1. precipitation with high levels of acidity

| | c | | d | | r | | | n |

2. another term for acid rain

| | c | | d | | d | | p | | s | | t | | | n |

3. solid acid deposition that settles on trees and buildings

| d | r | | | d | | p | | s | | t | | | n |

4. acid pollutants that reach the earth in precipitation

| w | | t | | d | | p | | s | | t | | | n |

5. a group of two or more atoms that acts like one atom

| r | | d | | c | | l |

6. neither an acid nor a base

| n | | | t | r | | l |

7. devices that remove sulfur from industrial smokestack emissions

| s | c | r | | b | b | | r | s |

Directions Decide whether each item describes an acid or a base.
Write *A* for acid and *B* for base.

_____ **8.** contains the hydroxyl (OH) radical

_____ **9.** a substance having a pH below 7

_____ **10.** a substance having a pH above 7

Climate Change

Directions Choose the term from the Word Bank that completes each sentence correctly. Write the answer on the line.

Word Bank	
carbon sequestration	greenhouse effect
carbon sink	greenhouse gases
climate change	

1. The change in Earth's climate due to global warming is called _____.

2. Gases in the atmosphere called _____ help trap heat against the earth.

3. The _____ warms the atmosphere because of trapped energy from the sun.

4. The long-term storage of carbon dioxide in forests, soils, oceans, and underground is called _____.

5. A _____ is a place where carbon accumulates and is stored.

Directions Answer each question on the lines. Use complete sentences.

6. How do worldwide increases in temperatures affect Earth's climate?

_____

_____

7. What has caused carbon dioxide levels to increase by almost one-third?

_____

_____

8. What is the main cause of greenhouse gases? _____

_____

9. How can countries reduce their emissions of greenhouse gases? _____

_____

10. What are two ways to increase carbon sequestration? _____

_____

Chapter 9 Vocabulary Review

Directions Choose the term from the Word Bank that completes each sentence correctly. Write the answer on the line.

Word Bank		
acid rain	catalytic converter	noise pollution
air pollutants	emission	smog
carbon sequestration	greenhouse gases	
carbon sink	neutral	

1. A haze that forms as a result of vehicle and industry emissions is called _____.

2. Gases in the atmosphere that trap heat against the earth are called _____.

3. A substance that is _____ has a pH of 7.

4. A(n) _____ is a place where carbon accumulates and is stored.

5. The long-term storage of carbon dioxide is known as _____.

6. Materials in the air that damage living and nonliving things are known as _____.

7. A(n) _____ is a device designed to reduce emissions of air pollutants from vehicles.

8. When noise interrupts daily life, it is called _____.

9. A(n) _____ is the release of a substance into the environment.

10. Precipitation with high levels of acidity is known as _____.

Chapter 9 Vocabulary Review, continued

Directions Match the items in Column A with those in Column B.
Write the letter of each correct answer on the line.

Column A

_____ **11.** harmful pollutants that are formed from
chemical reactions in the air

_____ **12.** increased temperatures in urban areas caused
by human activities

_____ **13.** group of two or more atoms that acts like one atom

_____ **14.** precipitation with high levels of acidity

_____ **15.** bitter, slippery substance that contains
hydroxyl radicals

_____ **16.** the result of pollutants produced primarily
by burning gasoline

_____ **17.** acidic pollutants that reach the earth as precipitation

_____ **18.** pollution in the air

_____ **19.** the scale used to measure whether a substance
is an acid or base

_____ **20.** acidic pollutants that settle on the earth as solids

_____ **21.** the warming of the atmosphere because of
trapped heat from the sun

_____ **22.** pollution that is formed and measured in
outdoor air

_____ **23.** related to breathing

_____ **24.** a haze produced by burning coal and oil

_____ **25.** pollution found and measured indoors

Column B

A acid deposition

B base

C radical

D secondary air pollutants

E urban heat island effect

F air pollution

G dry deposition

H pH

I photochemical smog

J wet deposition

K greenhouse effect

L indoor air pollution

M industrial smog

N outdoor air pollution

O respiratory

Chapter 9 Vocabulary Review, continued

Directions Read each statement. Circle the answer that correctly completes each sentence.

26. A harmful gas called (carbon dioxide, methane, ozone) is found in photochemical smog.

27. Devices that remove sulfur from industrial smokestack emissions are called (cleaners, scrubbers, purifiers).

28. A(n) (acid, base, oxide) is a sour-tasting substance that reacts with metals to produce hydrogen.

29. Bothersome brightness or glare from human-made lights is called (noise pollution, light pollution, glare pollution).

30. Solid or liquid particles in the air are called (pollutant matter, vapor, particulate matter).

31. A(n) (primary air pollutant, secondary air pollutant, indoor air pollutant) is a harmful chemical that enters the air directly.

32. Global (pollution, deposition, climate change) is a change in the earth's climate associated with global warming.

Introducing Solid Waste

Directions Write the letter of the answer that best completes each sentence.

1. Discarded materials, called _____, include items
   such as paper, scrap metal, and yard waste.
   A slag   **B** sludge   **C** fly ash   **D** solid waste

2. The process of how waste is created, collected, and disposed of is called the _____.
   A solid waste   **B** smelting waste   **C** waste stream   **D** fly ash

3. Toxic waste, also known as _____ waste, can harm people,
   wildlife, and the environment.
   A household   **B** hazardous   **C** environmental   **D** synthetic

4. Waste that can be broken down by living organisms is _____ waste.
   A biodegradable   **C** solid
   B nonbiodegradable   **D** synthetic

5. Waste that is _____ cannot be broken down by living organisms.
   A solid   **C** synthetic
   B hazardous   **D** nonbiodegradable

Directions Choose the term from the Word Bank that completes each sentence
correctly. Write the answer on the line.

Word Bank	
agricultural solid waste	slag
fly ash	sludge
industrial solid waste	

6. Semisolid leftovers from sewage treatment processes are called _____.

7. Waste ash, called _____, comes from coal-burning
   electrical power plants.

8. Leftover waste from making iron and other metals is _____.

9. Waste known as _____ comes from manufacturing
   and other industrial processes.

10. Solid waste from agriculture is _____.

Disposing of Solid Waste

Directions Read each statement. Circle the answer that correctly completes each sentence.

1. A(n) (open dump, sanitary landfill, incinerator) is a site specifically created for disposing of solid waste on land.

2. A metallic element that can damage living things is known as a (leachate, casing, heavy metal).

3. The natural breakdown of organic matter, called (aerobic decomposition, sanitation, land filling), requires water and oxygen.

4. A facility called a(n) (landfill, incinerator, leachate) is a place where waste is burned.

5. Contaminated water that leaks from a dump or landfill is called (slag, leachate, sludge).

6. A(n) (sanitary landfill, incinerator, open dump) is a place where garbage is dumped without environmental controls.

Directions Answer each question on the lines. Use complete sentences.

7. State one advantage and one disadvantage of sanitary landfills.

_____

_____

8. What are two disadvantages of using incinerators?

_____

_____

_____

9. How does the process of composting help the waste stream?

_____

_____

10. What is the process of recycling designed to do?

_____

_____

Hazardous Waste

Directions Use the terms in the Word Bank to complete the
paragraph. Write the terms on the lines.

Word Bank		
canisters	EPA	liquid
chemical	gas	PCBs
disposal	hazardous	solid

Many of the products people use create **1.** _____ waste.

Hazardous waste requires special methods of **2.** _____

so that it does less damage to the environment. Hazardous waste comes in many

different forms. It can be a **3.** _____, **4.** _____,

or a **5.** _____. It can be stored in barrels or

6. _____. Most of the country's hazardous waste is

generated by the **7.** _____ industry. At one time, toxic

8. _____ were used to make paint and electrical equipment.

The **9.** _____ oversees disposal of all toxic wastes.

Directions Unscramble the word in parentheses to complete each sentence.

10. The organisms in _____ waste can cause diseases.
(siuotcenif)

11. Waste that is _____ eats or wears away material by
chemical action. (ecvisoorr)

12. Hazardous waste that is _____ catches on fire easily.
(baeltiign)

13. A by-product of nuclear reactions is _____ waste.
(daoiartcevi)

14. Waste that can explode or give off toxic fumes is _____
waste. (caervite)

15. Copper, mercury, copper, and other _____ metals
are toxic. (eyhva)

Controlling Solid Waste

Directions Answer each question on the lines. Use complete sentences.

1. How will an increase in the world's population affect amounts of waste?

_____

_____

2. What is integrated waste management designed to do?

_____

_____

3. What are the "three Rs" for waste prevention? Briefly describe each one.

_____

_____

4. How does buying products with minimal packaging help the environment?

_____

_____

Directions Match the items in Column A with those in Column B.
Write the letter of each correct answer on the line.

Column A

_____ **5.** a dump designed specifically for hazardous waste

_____ **6.** a liquid that can dissolve other substances

_____ **7.** generating less waste

_____ **8.** carbon-based molecules

_____ **9.** process where toxic liquids are pumped into underground cracks

_____ **10.** combining many approaches to solving waste problems

Column B

A deep-well injection

B integrated waste management

C organic compounds

D secure chemical landfill

E solvent

F source reduction

Chapter 10 Vocabulary Review

Directions Match the items in Column A with those in Column B.
Write the letter of each correct answer on the line.

Column A

_____ 1. a mineral that contains metal

_____ 2. unstable waste that can explode or give off toxic fumes

_____ 3. waste from manufacturing and other industrial processes

_____ 4. able to be broken down by organisms

_____ 5. a process where toxic liquids are pumped into cracks in underground rock layers

_____ 6. where garbage is dumped without environmental controls

_____ 7. a by-product of nuclear reactions

_____ 8. how waste is created, collected, and disposed of

_____ 9. waste that can cause diseases

_____ 10. a metallic element that can damage living things

_____ 11. waste that can easily catch on fire

_____ 12. human-made

_____ 13. generating less waste

_____ 14. the breakdown of organic matter that requires water and oxygen

_____ 15. hazardous waste from households

Column B

A biodegradable

B deep-well injection

C industrial solid waste

D ore

E reactive waste

F heavy metal

G infectious waste

H open dump

I radioactive waste

J waste stream

K aerobic decomposition

L household hazardous waste

M ignitable waste

N source reduction

O synthetic

Chapter 10 Vocabulary Review, continued

Directions Write the letter of the answer that best completes each sentence.

16. A _____ is a liquid that can dissolve other substances.

   A solute   **B** dissolvent   **C** solution   **D** solvent

17. The process of removing metals from rocks through melting is called _____.

   A smelting   **B** mining   **C** recycling   **D** incinerating

18. Toxic chemicals called _____ were once used to make paint and other industrial products.

   A DEET   **B** PCBs   **C** DDTs   **D** CFCs

19. A(n) _____ is a facility where trash is burned.

   A oven   **B** smelter   **C** incinerator   **D** fireplace

20. Discarded solid materials are called _____.

   A biotic waste   **C** heavy metals

   B solid waste   **D** synthetic waste

21. Semisolid waste called _____ is left over from sewage treatment.

   A fly ash   **B** slag   **C** leachate   **D** sludge

22. Wastes that are _____ cannot be broken down by living organisms.

   A biodegradable   **C** radioactive

   B hazardous   **D** nonbiodegradable

23. Contaminated water known as _____ sometimes leaks from landfills.

   A sludge   **B** leachate   **C** slag   **D** runoff

24. Garbage produced by homes, businesses, and institutions is known as _____.

   A agricultural solid waste   **C** municipal solid waste

   B industrial solid waste   **D** reactive waste

25. A _____ is a site designed for disposing of solid waste on land.

   A sanitary landfill   **C** waste stream

   B deep-well injection   **D** decomposition site

Chapter 10 Vocabulary Review, continued

Directions Choose the term from the Word Bank that completes each sentence correctly. Write the answer on the line.

Word Bank	
agricultural solid waste	integrated waste management
corrosive	secure chemical landfill
fly ash	slag
hazardous waste	

26. The waste from making iron or other metals is known as _____.

27. Waste ash called _____ is released from coal-burning electrical power plants.

28. The use of a combination of approaches to control solid waste is known as _____.

29. A(n) _____ is a dump designed specifically for hazardous waste.

30. Toxic waste that can harm living things and the environment is called _____.

31. Waste that is _____ eats or wears away material by chemical action.

32. Solid waste from agriculture is called _____.

Agriculture and the Environment

Directions Choose the term from the Word Bank that completes each sentence correctly. Write the answer on the line.

Word Bank		
crop yield	feedlot	rangeland
dead zone	industrialized	soil erosion
domesticated	pasture	
draft animals	plantation	

1. An area of land used for livestock grazing is a(n) _____.

2. Large animals like horses and oxen used for pulling farm equipment are called _____.

3. The process of _____ moves soil from one place to another.

4. Animals bred for human use are referred to as being _____ animals.

5. A(n) _____ is an area of the ocean without anything living in it.

6. A confined area where large numbers of livestock are raised together is a(n) _____.

7. The size of the harvest from a particular crop is called the _____.

8. About 25 percent of Earth's grass-covered land is used for _____. Livestock graze on this land.

9. Large-scale agriculture is known as _____ agriculture.

10. In tropical areas, large-scale farms grow single crops in a process called _____ agriculture.

Protecting Soils

Directions Label each of the following as *OH* for O horizon or *AH* for A horizon.

_____ **1.** the top layer of the soil

_____ **2.** the second layer of the soil

_____ **3.** contains newly fallen and partially decayed leaves and twigs

_____ **4.** made up of decaying organic matter and inorganic particles

_____ **5.** also known as topsoil

Directions Match the items in Column A with those in Column B. Write the letter of each correct answer on the line.

Column A

_____ **6.** soil made up of clay, silt, and sand

_____ **7.** the buildup of soil in aquatic ecosystems

_____ **8.** planting rows of crops that curve around the contour of the land

_____ **9.** rows of planted trees that reduce wind erosion

_____ **10.** the percentage of a volume of soil that is empty space

Column B

A contour farming

B loam

C porosity

D shelterbelts

E siltation

_____ **11.** a layer of soil

_____ **12.** plowing up the soil before seeds are planted

_____ **13.** solid layer of rock beneath soil and other loose materials

_____ **14.** material from which soil first forms

_____ **15.** the process by which bedrock is broken down into smaller particles

F bedrock

G horizon

H parent material

I tilling

J weathering

World Food Supply and Nutrition

Directions Read each statement. Circle the answer that correctly completes each sentence.

1. A (protein, carbohydrate, fat) is a sugar or starch that living things use for energy.

2. A vitamin needed for health and growth is (iron, fat, vitamin C).

3. The (Green Revolution, world food supply, famine) increased crop yields by developing new varieties of plants.

4. A mineral that helps move oxygen through the bloodstream is (iron, vitamin C, calcium).

5. The growth of bones depends on (fat, calcium, vitamin C).

6. The (Green Revolution, Agricultural Revolution, world food supply) is the amount of food available for the world's population.

7. A blood condition called (anemia, overnutrition, vitamin A deficiency) can result from lack of iron.

8. Eating too many fats and sugars can result in (anemia, protein, overnutrition).

9. A chemical called (protein, vitamin C, fat) stores large amounts of energy.

Directions Write the letter of the answer that best completes each sentence.

10. A _____ is a chemical used by cells to grow and do work.

   A fat   **B** protein   **C** carbohydrate   **D** mineral

11. Something is _____ if it can be eaten safely.

   A edible   **B** concentrated   **C** overnutrition   **D** distributed

12. A _____ is equal to 1,000 calories.

   A famine   **B** protein   **C** kilocalorie   **D** fat

13. During a(n) _____, large numbers of people are hungry because of droughts or war.

   A famine   **B** Green Revolution   **C** overnutrition   **D** anemia

14. Not consuming enough fats, carbohydrates, or proteins leads to _____.

   A overnutrition   **B** famine   **C** hunger   **D** malnutrition

15. A _____ is a unit of heat needed to raise one gram of water one degree Celsius.

   A kilocalorie   **B** famine   **C** protein   **D** calorie

Sustainable Agriculture

Directions Choose the term from the Word Bank that completes each sentence correctly. Write the answer on the line.

Word Bank	
community-supported agriculture	industrialized agriculture
	organic farming
farmers market	sustainable agriculture

1. A(n) _____ is a place where local farmers can sell their produce.

2. In _____, produce is grown without the use of chemicals.

3. In _____, members pay a farm for deliveries of fresh produce.

4. A way to produce food for current generations without depriving future generations is called _____.

5. The practice of _____ raises a lot of animals in a small amount of space.

Directions Answer each question on the line. Use complete sentences.

6. Name one advantage and one disadvantage of organic farming.

_____

_____

7. What concerns might farmers consider when using a new pesticide?

_____

_____

8. How do predator insects act as natural pesticides?

_____

9. How does sun-grown coffee affect local environments?

_____

10. What is the goal of sustainable agriculture?

_____

Fisheries

Directions Complete the science terms by writing missing letters.
Use the clues to help you.

1. Fish farming is also called _____.

	q			c		l	t		r	e

2. Unwanted animals caught in fish nets are _____.

b		c		t		h

3. A net that floats freely through the ocean is known as a _____.

d			f	t		n		t

4. A _____ is a large net dragged through the ocean by a boat.

t			w	l		n		t

5. When fish are caught faster than they can reproduce, _____ occurs.

	v		r	f		s			n	

Directions Use the terms in the Word Bank to complete the
paragraph. Write the terms on the lines.

Word Bank	
animals	targeted
environmental	technologies
species	

Improved **6.** _____ have greatly increased fish

catches around the world. Unfortunately, these gains come with

7. _____ costs. For example, gill nets and longlines not

only catch the **8.** _____ fish. They also catch fish of the

wrong **9.** _____. They even catch other types of

10. _____, such as turtles, dolphins, and whales.

Chapter 11 Vocabulary Review

Directions Choose the term from the Word Bank that completes each sentence correctly. Write the answer on the line.

Word Bank		
anemia	feedlot	porosity
calorie	industrialized agriculture	siltation
draft animal		trawl net
farmers market	overfish	

1. Large numbers of livestock are raised together in a(n) _____.

2. When people _____, they catch fish faster than they can reproduce.

3. The buildup of soil in aquatic ecosystems is called _____.

4. A(n) _____ is an animal used to pull farm equipment.

5. Local farmers sell their produce at a(n) _____.

6. A(n) _____ is a net that is dragged through the ocean.

7. The _____ of soil is percentage of its volume that is empty space.

8. A blood condition called _____ can result from a lack of iron.

9. A(n) _____ is the heat needed to raise a gram of water one degree Celsius.

10. Large-scale agriculture is known as _____.

Chapter 11 Vocabulary Review, continued

Directions Use the terms in the Word Bank to complete the
paragraphs. Write the terms on the lines.

Word Bank		
A horizon	horizons	parent material
bedrock	O horizon	weathering

Soil exists in several layers, which are called **11.** _____.

The top layer is called the **12.** _____, which contains

leaves, twigs, and other organic matter. The next layer of soil is the

13. _____, otherwise known as topsoil. Many of the

minerals found in soil originated deep below the topsoil. Most soil is formed

from the breakdown, or **14.** _____, of larger pieces of

15. _____. This material often originates from a solid

layer below all of the soil layers. This layer of solid rock is known as

16. _____.

Word Bank		
calcium	fats	proteins
carbohydrates	iron	vitamin C

In order to be healthy, people must have a well-balanced diet with certain

components. People need three main forms of foods in their diets. The first are

17. _____, which are chemicals found in meat and meat

products. People also need to take in a certain amount of

18. _____, which store energy. The energy that human

bodies need to function comes from **19.** _____. Sources

of these sugars and starches include breads, cereals, fruits, and vegetables.

Chapter 11 Vocabulary Review, continued

The three main types of foods contain nutrients that help the body to function.

The mineral **20.** _____ is needed to carry oxygen

through the blood. Another important mineral is **21.** _____,

which helps to build up bones, teeth, and muscles. An important vitamin

called **22.** _____ helps to support health and

growth. If people do not consume enough of these essential nutrients, their

bodies cannot function properly.

Directions Match the items in Column A with those in Column B. Write the letter
of each correct answer on the line.

Column A	**Column B**
_____ **23.** to plow soil before planting seeds	**A** crop yield
_____ **24.** the size of a harvest from a particular crop	**B** drift net
_____ **25.** a net that floats freely through the ocean	**C** edible
_____ **26.** able to be eaten safely	**D** longline
_____ **27.** a long cable with baited hooks every few meters	**E** till
_____ **28.** land used for livestock grazing	**F** bycatch
_____ **29.** too young to reproduce	**G** community-supported agriculture
_____ **30.** rows of trees to reduce wind erosion of soil	
_____ **31.** unwanted fish	**H** immature
_____ **32.** where members pay to receive deliveries of fresh produce from a farm	**I** pasture
	J shelterbelts

Chapter 11 Vocabulary Review, continued

Column A

_____ **33.** single crops grown on a large scale, usually in tropical locations

_____ **34.** the amount of food available for the world's population

_____ **35.** net that traps a fish's head

_____ **36.** an area in the ocean without any living organisms

_____ **37.** where crops curve around the contours of the land

_____ **38.** grass-covered land where animals graze

_____ **39.** bred for human use

_____ **40.** ways of producing food without depriving future generations

_____ **41.** not consuming enough fats, carbohydrates, or protein

_____ **42.** an increase in crop yields by developing new varieties of plants

Column B

K contour farming

L dead zone

M gill net

N plantation agriculture

O world food supply

P domesticated

Q Green Revolution

R protein-calorie malnutrition

S rangeland

T sustainable agriculture

Directions Read each statement. Circle the answer that correctly completes each sentence.

43. A soil called (loam, silt, bedrock) is best for growing crops.

44. When produce is grown without using chemicals, it is called (plantation agriculture, organic farming, community-supported agriculture).

45. A (drought, flood, famine) is when large numbers of people in an area are hungry due to a disaster or war.

46. The movement of soil from one place to another is (soil depletion, soil erosion, overgrazing).

47. Fish farming is called (aquaculture, fishery, overfishing).

48. When people eat too many calories it is called (malnutrition, anemia, overnutrition).

Chapter 11 Vocabulary Review, continued

49. A (megacalorie, kilocalorie, millicalorie) is 1,000 calories.

50. In (contour farming, no-till farming, organic farming), the soil is left undisturbed until a new crop is planted.

51. Farmers who produce (draft animals, loam, shade-grown coffee) do so without clearing tropical forests.

52. In (contour farming, clear-cutting, weathering), all of the trees in a large area are harvested.

Major Threats to Biodiversity

Directions The letters below stand for the five major reasons for the
loss of biodiversity. On the lines, write what each letter stands for.

1. H _____

2. I _____

3. P _____

4. P _____

5. O _____

Directions Read each statement. Circle the answer that correctly
completes each sentence.

6. An organism brought to an area where it is not naturally found is called
a(n) (native species, introduced species, found organism).

7. When (wildlife trade, species introduction, habitat fragmentation) occurs,
large areas of habitat are broken up into smaller areas.

8. A(n) (acronym, regulation, fragmentation) is a word formed
from the first letters of other words.

9. Any sale of wildlife or wildlife products is known as
(habitat fragmentation, introduced species, wildlife trade).

10. A giant asteroid slamming into Earth would raise an enormous
cloud of (trees, gas, dust).

11. Scientists believe there have been (nine, five, six) mass extinctions
in the past.

12. Unlike extinctions in the past, (weather disturbances, ice flows, human
activities) are the biggest cause of current extinctions.

13. The biggest threat to biodiversity is (habitat loss, lack of food,
greenhouse gases).

14. Many types of (food, ecosystems, pollution) can cause problems
for biodiversity.

15. Some scientists estimate that the earth is currently losing more than
(100,000, 5,000, 30,000) species a year.

Disappearing Habitat

Directions Choose the term from the Word Bank that completes each sentence correctly. Write the answer on the line.

1. Deforestation and _____ are two main causes of habitat loss.

2. Many North American forests are still being _____ or developed.

3. Scientists estimate that more than 70 percent of all _____ are caused by habitat loss.

4. The mating of related individuals is _____.

5. Forests that have trees that are more than 150 years old are _____.

Word Bank
development
extinctions
inbreeding
logged
old-growth forests

Directions Answer each question on the lines. Use complete sentences.

6. What are three types of development that cause the loss of rain forests?

   _____

   _____

7. What can happen to species when their natural habitats are lost?

   _____

   _____

8. What area shelters more than one-third of Earth's species?

   _____

   _____

9. How did the Aral Sea in Central Asia decrease in size?

   _____

   _____

10. How are some countries working to prevent habitat loss?

   _____

   _____

Introduced Species

Directions Use the terms in the Word Bank to complete the paragraph.
Write the terms on the lines.

Word Bank	
economic	human
ecosystem	predators
exotic	

An introduced species is one that is introduced into a new **1.** _____.

Introduced species are also called **2.** _____ or invasive species.

These organisms do not have **3.** _____ in their new homes.

Their introduction can cause **4.** _____ and environmental harm.

Introduced species can also harm **5.** _____ health.

Directions Answer each question on the lines. Use complete sentences.

6. What is a hatchery?

_____

_____

7. Why did people bring kudzu into the United States?

_____

8. What problems did kudzu cause when it was introduced?

_____

_____

9. What are two ways that nonnative species can be accidentally introduced?

_____

_____

10. What is the most serious threat of an introduced species?

_____

_____

Wildlife Trade

Directions Complete the chart. In the last column, write *E* for Ecological View, *U* for Utilitarian View, *R* for Recreational View, or *S* for Spiritual View.

Reasons for protecting biodiversity	View
Natural areas provide opportunities for outdoor activities.	**1.** _____
Biodiversity provides many products.	**2.** _____
Ecosystems and the services they provide are important.	**3.** _____
All species have a purpose in life.	**4.** _____

Directions Use the terms in the Word Bank to complete the paragraph. Write the terms on the lines.

The **5.** _____ is the largest importer of wildlife products. A growing amount of wildlife trade is **6.** _____. People are **7.** _____, buying, and selling **8.** _____ or threatened species. Illegal trade in wildlife has pushed many species to the point of **9.** _____. Rhinoceroses are hunted for their **10.** _____, which are used to make medicines. Tigers are hunted for their beautiful **11.** _____. Elephants have been hunted for their valuable ivory **12.** _____. People who hunt wildlife illegally are called **13.** _____. When the **14.** _____ for wildlife products is strong, prices rise. People are more willing to break the law when they will be **15.** _____.

Word Bank

demand

endangered

extinction

fur

horns

hunting

illegal

poachers

tusks

United States

well paid

Protecting Biodiversity for the Future

Directions Answer each question on the lines. Use complete sentences.

1. What is the purpose of the Endangered Species Act?

_____

_____

2. What is the purpose of ecological restoration?

_____

_____

3. Why do people feel it is important to protect and restore the Everglades?

_____

_____

4. What does CITES stand for?

_____

_____

5. What is the goal of the Treaty on Biological Diversity?

_____

_____

Directions Unscramble the words in parentheses to complete each sentence.
Write the terms on the lines.

6. Seed banks are large _____ of seeds. (tcelcolnois)

7. Many countries have laws that protect _____. (vidboirseyit)

8. Zoos, aquariums, and botanical gardens help _____
threatened and endangered species. (creptto)

9. Everglades National Park is a unique _____ in
southern Florida. (dwtenla)

10. In almost every part of the United States, habitat _____
is taking place. (aoroitntrse)

Chapter 12 Vocabulary Review

Directions Write the letter of the answer that best completes each sentence.

1. Fish eggs are hatched in a(n) _____.

  A hatchery   **B** nursery   **C** incubator   **D** fish farm

2. A(n) _____ is brought into an area where it is not found naturally.

  A foreign specimen   **B** transplant   **C** introduced species **D** trade species

3. The acronym _____ stands for the five major reasons for biodiversity loss.

  A RHINO   **B** HIPPO   **C** HAPPY   **D** GATOR

4. People with a(n)_____ believe that every living thing has a purpose.

  A ecological view   **C** recreational view

  B utilitarian view   **D** spiritual view

5. Areas of cover that connect isolated habitat are called _____.

  A habitat connectors   **C** tree belts

  B patch links   **D** wildlife corridors

6. Those with a(n) _____ view want to protect biodiversity because of beneficial products.

  A recreational   **B** utilitarian   **C** spiritual   **D** ecological

Directions Match the items in Column A with those in Column B.
Write the letter of each correct answer on the line.

Column A	Column B
_____ **7.** buying or selling wildlife or wildlife products	**A** acronym
_____ **8.** a view that natural areas should be preserved for outdoor activities	**B** asteroid
_____ **9.** a word formed from the first letters of other words	**C** ecological view
_____ **10.** a view that biodiversity should be protected to preserve ecosystems	**D** recreational view
_____ **11.** this may have slammed into the earth, causing a mass extinction	**E** wildlife trade

Chapter 12 Vocabulary Review, continued

Directions Chose the term from the Word Bank that completes each sentence correctly. Write the answer on the line.

Word Bank	
captive breeding	malaria
ecological restoration	poacher
habitat fragmentation	seed bank
inbreeding	sustainable development

12. The mating of related individuals is _____.

13. Seeds of endangered species are stored in a(n) _____.

14. The process of repairing damage to an ecosystem
is _____.

15. A(n) _____ is someone who hunts wildlife illegally.

16. Breeding plants or animals in zoos, aquariums, or botanical gardens
is _____.

17. In _____, large habitats are broken into
smaller pieces.

18. Mosquitoes can be carriers of _____.

19. The Treaty on Biological Diversity supports _____.

Understanding Sustainability

Directions Write the letter of the answer that best completes each sentence.

1. The people of Easter Island are an example of a(n) _____ society.

   A sustainable   **B** threatened   **C** poor   **D** unsustainable

2. To _____ means to express something as a number.

   A subtract   **B** conserve   **C** sustain   **D** quantify

3. A global plan for sustainability developed at the Earth Summit is known as _____.

   A the Clean Water Act   **C** Agenda 21
   B the Endangered Species Act   **D** the Environmental Plan

4. A(n) _____ is a measure of change.

   A indicator   **B** democracy   **C** plan   **D** treaty

5. Environmental _____ can help people understand and value a sustainable way of life.

   A industry   **B** education   **C** technology   **D** profits

Directions Use the terms in the Word Bank to complete the paragraph.
Write the terms on the lines.

People today have an advantage over the inhabitants of Easter Island. They have

6. _____ to help them see what has happened in the past.

They can act on this information to create a more sustainable future. The things

that are important to people are their **7.** _____. Many

people have strong environmental values. They want to develop a sustainable

future. There are three main goals of **8.** _____. The first

goal is **9.** _____ health. This includes conserving natural

resources, **10.** _____ natural systems, and protecting

11. _____. The second goal is **12.** _____

health, which includes economic **13.** _____ or growth.

The third goal is **14.** _____ health. This includes supporting

basic human needs as well as sustainable practices in the community. Different

indicators can be used to determine people's **15.** _____

in meeting these three goals.

Word Bank
biodiversity
ecological
economic
preserving
records
social
stability
success
sustainability
values

A Sustainable Global Economy

Directions Match the items in Column A with those in Column B.
Write the letter of each correct answer on the line.

Column A

_____ **1.** a measure of progress that includes economic, social, and environmental factors

_____ **2.** an expert in the field of economics

_____ **3.** the total value of all goods and services produced in a country in a given period of time

_____ **4.** an economist who works to account for nature's value in economics

_____ **5.** wealth that is used to generate more wealth

_____ **6.** natural resources that produce a flow of goods and services

_____ **7.** an economy that contributes to the sustainability of the earth

Column B

A economist

B environmental economist

C financial capital

D genuine progress indicator

E gross domestic product

F natural capital

G sustainable global economy

Directions Choose the term from the Word Bank that completes each sentence correctly. Write the answer on the line.

8. For people interested in sustainability, the GDP is not a very good indicator of _____.

9. Many people are trying to develop new _____ of economic progress.

10. The GPI also includes things like _____ as gains.

11. Some experts say the new indicators are too _____.

12. One goal of sustainability is to achieve economic _____.

13. The GDP does not reflect all social and _____ problems.

14. Defenders of the new economic indicators say that they _____ many factors the GDP ignores.

15. Although people value the parts of the natural world, they are not required to _____ for them.

Word Bank

ecological

include

measures

pay

progress

strength

subjective

volunteering

Sustainable Communities

Directions Choose the term from the Word Bank that completes each sentence correctly. Write the answer on the line.

1. Traveling in cars leads to increased air pollution, traffic _____, and road building.

2. Walking and _____ are two good options for reducing pollution and automobile traffic.

3. In Devil's Lake, North Dakota, wastewater is treated in a facility that contains _____ plants.

4. A(n) _____ is ridden by people who live in the suburbs and work in the city.

5. A(n) _____ is a place and the people and other organisms that live there.

6. Wherever people live, they create a built _____.

7. Sprawl can lead to more travel, using more _____ fuels and other natural resources.

Word Bank
aquatic
biking
community
commuter train
congestion
environment
fossil

8. Low-density, unplanned suburban development is _____.

9. Communities that surround cities are known as _____.

10. Buses and subways are forms of _____.

11. Some communities support more renewable forms of energy by building _____ farms.

12. A(n) _____ is built around the ideas of sustainability.

13. A line around a city past which no new development can occur is known as a(n) _____.

Word Bank
public transportation
sprawl
suburbs
sustainable community
urban growth boundary
wind

Directions Answer each question on the lines. Use complete sentences.

14. How do city buildings help peregrine falcons? _____

_____

15. How are jobs part of a sustainable community? _____

_____

Government, Science, Business, and Citizens

Directions Read each statement. Circle the answer that correctly completes each statement.

1. One of the most important actions you can take to express your views is (working, voting, leaving).

2. Volunteer work, such as (citizen science projects, composting, industry), helps researchers solve real-world problems.

3. In (citizen science projects, politics, corporate social responsibility), businesses contribute to a cleaner environment.

4. A (research project, community resource, regulatory agency) enforces laws and regulations.

5. A plan of action for political issues is a (policy, regulation, law).

6. A rule enforced by a government agency is referred to as a (policy, regulation, business).

7. By making more environmentally friendly consumer choices, you can have a (negative, positive, corporate) impact on the environment.

8. The EPA helps (fund, protect, enforce) environmental laws and regulations.

9. Scientists provide important information to (lawmakers, criminals, architects) so that they can make informed decisions.

10. Many car companies are making (bigger, hybrid, smaller) cars that get much better gas mileage.

11. Rachel Carson helped create awareness about the problems with (weather, floods, pesticides).

12. Products with a lot of (weight, packaging, chemicals) increase the amount of solid waste.

13. People can get involved in environmental activities such as creating trails and getting rid of (ugly, large, nonnative) plants.

14. In a (democracy, city, republic), voting is an important right and responsibility.

15. Corporations know that many (companies, consumers, industries) are buying with the environment in mind.

Chapter 13 Vocabulary Review

Directions Chose the term from the Word Bank that completes each sentence correctly. Write the answer on the line.

Word Bank	
citizen science projects	policy
commuter train	regulation
corporate social responsibility	urban growth boundary
genuine progress indicator	

1. A(n) _____ is a rule enforced by a government agency.

2. The role of business in helping society and the environment is _____.

3. The _____ includes economic, social, and environmental factors.

4. New development around a city cannot occur past the _____.

5. A(n) _____ is a plan of action for political issues.

6. In _____, volunteers work with scientists to answer real-world questions.

7. People who travel regularly from the suburbs to the city may ride a(n) _____.

Directions Match the items in Column A with those in Column B. Write the letter of each correct answer on the line.

Column A	Column B
_____ **8.** the total value of all goods and services in a country	**A** environmental economist
_____ **9.** a community built around the idea of sustainability	**B** financial capital
_____ **10.** buses and subways	**C** gross domestic product
_____ **11.** wealth that is used to generate more wealth	**D** natural capital
_____ **12.** an economist who works to demonstrate nature's value in economics	**E** public transportation
	F sustainable community
_____ **13.** natural resources that produce a flow of goods and services	**G** sustainable global economy
_____ **14.** an economy that contributes to the sustainability of the earth	

Chapter 13 Vocabulary Review, continued

Directions Unscramble the word or words in parenthesis to complete each sentence. Write the answer on the line.

15. A(n) _____ is a measure of change. (nicdatori)

16. Communities that surround cities are known
as _____. (busrusb)

17. A(n)_____ is an expert in the field of
economics. (monicotes)

18. Low-density, unplanned suburban development
is _____. (pawlrs)

19. To _____ something is to express it
as a number. (faqituyn)

20. A(n) _____ is a government agency that enforces
laws and regulations. (rotagyrelu necagy)